Creating a Vibrant
City Center

Urban Design and Regeneration Principles

Cy Paumier

Urban Land Institute

ULI–the Urban Land Institute

ULI–the Urban Land Institute is a nonprofit research and education organization that promotes responsible leadership in the use of land in order to enhance the total environment.

The Institute maintains a membership representing a broad spectrum of interests and sponsors a wide variety of educational programs and forums to encourage an open exchange of ideas and sharing of experience. ULI initiates research that anticipates emerging land use trends and issues and proposes creative solutions based on that research; provides advisory services; and publishes a wide variety of materials to disseminate information on land use and development.

Established in 1936, the Institute today has more than 20,000 members and associates from nearly 70 countries, representing the entire spectrum of the land use and development disciplines. Professionals represented include developers, builders, property owners, investors, architects, public officials, planners, real estate brokers, appraisers, attorneys, engineers, financiers, academics, students, and librarians. ULI relies heavily on the experience of its members. It is through member involvement and information resources that ULI has been able to set standards of excellence in development practice. The Institute has long been recognized as one of America's most respected and widely quoted sources of objective information on urban planning, growth, and development.

Richard M. Rosan
President

For more information about ULI and the resources that it offers related to city centers and a variety of other real estate and urban development issues, visit ULI's Web site at www.uli.org.

ULI Project Staff

Rachelle L. Levitt
Executive Vice President, Policy and Practice
Publisher/Project Manager

Gayle Berens
Vice President, Real Estate Development
    Practice

Nancy H. Stewart
Director, Book Program

James A. Mulligan
Managing Editor/Manuscript Editor

Betsy VanBuskirk
Art Director

Patrick Mullaly/pm Graphic Design
Book Design/Layout

Diann Stanley-Austin
Director, Publishing Operations

Recommended bibliographic listing:

Paumier, Cy. *Creating a Vibrant City Center: Urban Design and Regeneration Principles.* Washington, D.C.: ULI–the Urban Land Institute, 2004.

ULI Catalog Number: C63
International Standard Book Number: 0-87420-902-1

Copyright 2004 by ULI–the Urban Land Institute
1025 Thomas Jefferson Street, N.W.
Suite 500 West
Washington, D.C. 20007-5201

Cover photograph:

Bryant Park in New York City. William H. Whyte, program consultant; Laurie D. Olin, urban designer. Photographer: James B. Abbott.

Sponsors

ULI would like to thank the following companies and foundations for their generous sponsorship, which has permitted us to publish this book in full color:

The Herzfeld Foundation
Milwaukee, Wisconsin

Hines and Archstone-Smith
Washington, D.C.

The HNTB Corporation
Kansas City, Missouri

The Rouse Company
Columbia, Maryland

Warren Charitable Fund
Denver, Colorado

Review Committee

Acknowledgments

Many people contributed their time and talents to researching, writing, editing, and producing *Creating a Vibrant City Center*. Although it is not possible to mention everyone who participated in the production of this book, a number of individuals deserve special recognition and thanks.

Appreciation is due first to Connie Dimond and Scott Ditch, who did the original work translating the urban design principles and guidelines into manuscript form. This revised and updated second edition reflects the professional critique and input of Henry Alinger, Karla Brookes, David Holden, Kimberly Paumier, and Patrick Phillips. The overall design and layout of this publication evolved from a collaboration with Patrick Mullaly, a creative and talented graphic designer. The refinements and revisions to the manuscript were organized and recorded by Diana Morraye, my administrative assistant.

My urban design partners and colleagues who participated in preparing the city center development strategies deserve recognition for their professional contributions and commitment. Donald Hilderbrandt, Andy Kalback, Gary Maule, Craig Watson, and Keith Weaver were responsible for the design of the city center projects illustrated in this document. Professional leadership and support for the LDR urban design studio were provided by my partners John Hall, Fred Jarvis, Kipp Shrack, and Bert Winterbottom.

The faculty and professors at Ohio State University and the Harvard Graduate School of Design first stimulated my interest in the field of urban design.

The design principles and strategies defined in this book evolved from consultation and collaboration with several outstanding urban planners, among them Edmund Bacon, William Johnson, Hideo Sasaki, Bernard Weissbourd, and William Whyte, from whom I attained my knowledge and understanding of the complex economic, social, and physical changes taking place in our cities. The public and private clients who retained our services also deserve recognition for the challenging assignments they provided us in their cities. Special appreciation goes to the professionals who collaborated with us to design and implement a number of important urban projects: Nick Arnold, Rich Bradley, Al Copp, James Edwards, William Haberman, Michael Hayes, James Norton, Duncan Sutherland, and Jack Tuttle.

My sincere thanks and appreciation go to James Mulligan, whose editing shaped the book and helped make it user friendly, and to Rachelle Levitt and the ULI staff, who provided their professional insight, encouragement, and commitment to the publication of this book. The seven people on the ULI Review Committee also provided valuable input on and critique of the manuscript.

The greatest support for the preparation of this book came from my wife, Eunie, who accompanied me as I spent many vacations visiting and photographing cities, and my daughters, Kimberly, Terri, and Tami, who challenged my views on how to create more livable cities.

Cy Paumier

About the Author

Cy Paumier is an urban design consultant for the Downtown DC Business Improvement District (BID) in Washington, D.C. Paumier is also a senior urban design adviser with HNTB Corporation. Since 2002, he has been engaged in the preparation of a five-year public realm improvement plan for the parks, squares, streets, and boulevards in the 120-block BID area. This plan and the related implementation strategy are being developed in collaboration with the National Park Service, the District of Columbia Office of Planning, the National Capital Planning Commission, and BID property owners.

As national director of urban design for HNTB and a cofounder and principal of LDR International, now an HNTB company, Paumier contributed to the formulation of urban design plans for city center projects that enhance the built environment. The planning and vision-building process that he managed at HNTB and LDR for 30 years was effective in stimulating public and private investment in more than 50 cities in the United States and the United Kingdom. By creating a high-quality public realm, these plans have allowed people to satisfy their desire to live, work, shop, and relax in the heart of the city.

A commitment to invest time and resources in research and education was a hallmark of the founding partners of Land Design/Research, which became LDR International. The educational documents written and published by LDR were inspired by its many clients. For instance, *New Life for Maryland's Old Towns*, a report that focused on the reinvestment potential of the historic towns of Maryland, was sponsored by the Maryland Historical Trust in 1979.

The urban design principles and plans that evolved from working with clients in Savannah, Georgia; Baltimore, Maryland; and Washington, D.C., were presented to the Urban Land Institute to foster interest in publishing a book on city center design. A three-year collaboration with ULI culminated in the 1988 publication of *Designing the Successful Downtown*, which defined the principles and strategies that were inspiring confidence and faith in the city center regeneration process occurring in the United States. Publication of this planning and design document created many opportunities to participate in educational programs and conferences in the United States and abroad. The knowledge and experience gained on these occasions from interaction with professional leaders from around the world is reflected in this new edition.

Before his association with LDR and HNTB, Paumier was chief land planner for the Rouse Company, which developed the new town of Columbia, Maryland. He also provided design leadership for the development of Nuns' Island, a 1,000-acre residential community in Montreal; the Woodlands new town outside Houston; and the town center in Reston, Virginia.

Cy Paumier received a bachelor's degree from Ohio State University and a master's degree from the Harvard Graduate School of Design.

Contents

Foreword

The history of civilized man is, in essence, the history of cities. For centuries, cities have represented mankind's highest aspirations and nurtured its finest achievements. The concentration, diversity, and complexity of great cities generate intellectual energy and prosperity that, in turn, create civilization: architecture and the arts, science, religion, commerce, and politics.

Each city is unique—the expression of its diverse peoples, cultures, environment, and history. And because a city is so complex, it is inevitable that there will be cycles of decline and regeneration. The city's expression of itself is best personified at its core or center.

This book is about creating vibrant city centers. It is about the "what" and the "how." It is about places, but, more important, about principles and processes drawn from more than 45 years of experience. Today, most cities that have been successful in the revitalization of their centers have embraced a process that is both open and inclusive, providing people with the opportunity to offer valuable insight and input.

Today, these open and inclusive processes appear to be an example of democracy at its best—often with little regulation and a focus on consensus building. They start with a vision-building process open to the community in the form of workshops and charrettes. Common goals and objectives are identified. Illustrations of potential uses and activities are created to serve as a guide for future actions. Alliances are forged among various interests committed to implementation.

The planning and design process begins with an analysis of assets and opportunities. It is a time to "look, listen, and learn" from stakeholder meetings, public workshops, and steering committees. What is discovered is that each city is unique. Through an inventory of strengths and needs and identification of social, economic, and cultural character, the city center's intrinsic qualities become evident.

Every city has the potential for greatness. Unlocking the inherent qualities that are uniquely expressive of a particular city center provides the basis for the creation of memorable places, invigorating or restful spaces, and enriching environments. The health of the city center is critical to the broader economic development of a city and the region it serves. City leaders and decision makers must continue to share a commitment to sensitive design, high-quality development, and economic pragmatism.

As you read on, the way forward becomes self-evident.

Donald F. Hilderbrandt, FASLA
Design Director
HNTB Urban Design + Planning

Dedication

This book is dedicated to my father, Cyril Paumier, Sr., who taught me to appreciate the natural beauty in the urban landscape; to Floyd Stahl, my basketball coach at Ohio State University, who encouraged me to attend graduate school at Harvard University; to Edmund Bacon, who introduced me to the field of urban design; and to Bernard Weissbourd, who provided the professional opportunities required to support the founding of LDR International in 1969.

Creating a Vibrant City Center

The image of a great city stems largely from the quality of its public realm—its streets, boulevards, parks, squares, plazas, and waterfronts.

—Cy Paumier

Introduction

After decades of distress and uncertainty, city centers are reclaiming their prominence as the focus of business, culture, and entertainment. The abundance of life, color, variety, and surprise makes cities the place to go to seek and discover, to entertain and be entertained, to see and be seen, to meet, learn, and enjoy. As a home to millions of people and an attraction for numerous visitors, the city center facilitates a wonderful human chemistry. Cities create special settings for entertainment and tourism and have the potential to stimulate local and regional economies.

The image of a great city stems largely from the quality of its public realm—its streets, boulevards, parks, squares, plazas, and waterfronts. Individual architectural landmarks may become icons, but it is the quality of the overall public environment that makes a city livable and memorable. A well-designed and well-managed public realm evokes community pride and creates a strong, positive image. This environment, in conjunction with a strong and diversified economic marketplace, attracts the development investment needed to sustain and enhance the economic and social heart of the city.

Trafalgar Square, London.

Creating a Vibrant City Center sets forth planning and urban design principles and strategies centered on two characteristics that are key to the success of a city center:

❖ *A diverse market.* A city's unique character is defined by the diversity and concentration of complementary uses. These uses generate pedestrian activity and a lively social environment that, in turn, sustain the mix of uses.

❖ *A high-quality place.* A visually appealing, comfortable, and secure physical environment will create confidence, commitment, and investment in the community over the long term.

These two characteristics are closely linked and need to make equal contributions in order for successful city center regeneration to occur. The mix of uses should be analyzed to identify urban functions and activities that are missing or scarce. A program to retain or attract the desired mix of uses and amenities then can be undertaken

Bryant Park, New York City.

4

Morrison Street, Portland, Oregon.

offering financial and/or other incentives in order to obtain an appropriate balance of uses and activities.

In conjunction with marketing and economic development initiatives, a city needs to improve its public infrastructure, including streetscapes, plazas, parks and public spaces, signage, lighting, public transit, vehicular circulation, and parking. Of equal importance are the preservation and rehabilitation of significant buildings and a commitment to architectural design excellence for new structures.

Over the past 20 years, people have become increasingly aware of the economic and social benefits associated with well-planned improvements to the public realm. In Portland, Oregon, for example, creation of a pedestrian-friendly environment helped to spur significant private investment in residential, office, and retail development. The methods and processes used to design, build, and maintain Portland's city center provide an excellent case study of how creation of a high-quality public realm can be a

catalyst for regeneration throughout the city and the region.

The importance and value of place making and creating a high-quality environment have become more apparent to real estate professionals and community leaders committed to developing vibrant city centers, helping to fuel the growth of the city center housing market.

North Michigan Avenue, Chicago.

CIBC Bank Plaza, Toronto, Canada.

Strong partnerships between the local government and the private business community have led to some of the most successful and innovative improvements to city centers. Business improvement districts (BIDs) are demonstrating the importance of strong management structures and community involvement in addressing and solving the most salient city center issues: public realm maintenance, security, and marketing. Cities throughout the world are recognizing the need to create public/private partnerships to manage city center development and regeneration.

Trafalgar Square, London.

Champs-Elysées, Paris.

Great cities have not evolved by accident, nor do they conform to a single planning template. This second edition of *Creating a Vibrant City Center* identifies the principles and guidelines inherent in successful place making so they can be applied to cities of any scale. Building on the research and urban design work of the author in more than 50 cities in the United States, the United Kingdom, Europe, and Australia, this new edition provides guidance for how to develop comprehensive action programs for city center regeneration.

Marienplatz, Munich, Germany.

7

The parks of Washington are among the most beautiful in the world.

—Washington Post, *1903*

CHAPTER 1

Historical Perspective

From the 18th century to the middle of the 20th century, the city center was the focus of a region's economic and social life, where people came together to produce and trade goods and services, to meet, and to exchange information and ideas. It was a civic and cultural center and a symbol of community identity. Although social and economic forces have changed the city center's physical form and function, the same qualities inherent in cities of the past are critical to their success today. The new wave of city center regeneration is an attempt to re-create an environment that has long typified urban life. This chapter provides a historical look at the qualities that shape city centers.

Defining Characteristics

Certain characteristics of center cities made them places where people would gather, conduct business, shop, and live. Among these characteristics were accessibility, diversity of uses, concentration and intensity of use, and organizing structure.

Sherman Square, Washington, D.C.

Pennsylvania Avenue, Washington, D.C.'s grand avenue, was planned by Pierre L'Enfant in 1791 as the ceremonial boulevard connecting the two seats of power— the Congress House, or the Capitol, and the President's House, now known as the White House. By 1927, Pennsylvania Avenue had become Washington's "Main Street," with fashionable hotels, theaters, government offices, and retail shops.

Accessibility

The traditional city center was the hub of the regional transportation network. As long as the city center had superior road, water, and/or rail access, it provided a competitive advantage for manufacturing and business activities, creating a business concentration that generated substantial investment and a healthy economy. As long as "foot power" and horsepower served as primary modes of transportation, most city center functions had to be within a short distance of one another. With home and the workplace needing to be relatively close together, the traditional center was an important residential and business location, with neighborhoods accommodating residents of all socioeconomic levels.

Diversity of Uses

This need for proximity resulted in a rich and highly diverse mix of people and activities. Not only were there clusters of shops and stores capitalizing on the strategic location to serve nearby residents and businesses, but also the city center was the location for government offices, courts, schools, and cultural institutions. This rich mixture of city center uses created an economic vitality that encouraged the development of an increasing number of specialized functions. As long as the mix was rich and varied, the loss or failure of any one element was not likely to harm the economy as a whole. However, many cities became too reliant on the industrial sector, leaving them without adequate business diversity, which contributed to the decline of many city centers.

F Street, Washington's primary retail corridor, prospered as the hub for finer stores, restaurants, and movie theaters. The rich mix of city center uses created a high level of pedestrian activity and the market for development of specialized retail and commercial functions.

Overlapping spheres of business, shopping, home, and leisure pursuits put people on the same streets for different purposes at different times of the day. The resulting constant cycle and volume of pedestrian activity created a critical mass of potential users and consumers whose movements formed a web of mutually supportive relationships. The traditional city center's multiple-use character and high level of pedestrian activity also made it a rich social setting. The mix of uses ensured that there were opportunities for informal encounters and increased the convenience of meetings and social engagements. Thus, the central area became an important focus for personal interaction, helping to encourage the exchange of information and ideas that enhanced the economic and social vitality of the city.

Concentration and Intensity of Use

The intensity of development in the traditional central area was relatively high due to the value of land. Maximizing site coverage meant building close to the street, which created a strong sense of spatial enclosure. Although city center development was dense, construction practices limited building height and preserved a human scale. The consistency in building height and massing reinforced the pedestrian scale of streets, as well as the city center's architectural harmony and visual coherence.

The life and vitality of the historic marketplace was directly related to the pedestrian scale of the city's streets and public spaces. Many successful retail areas have preserved and enhanced these streets and public spaces that people find so enjoyable in city centers.

11

Market Square in Washington was designed to provide space for outdoor activities and special events. The retail shops, produce vendors, and activities that occurred in this central space attracted people from residential neighborhoods throughout the city.

frontage was keen. Development parcels were normally much deeper than they were wide, creating a pattern of relatively narrow building fronts that provided variety and articulation in each block and continuous activity on the street. The ground level was the best location for commercial uses, with upper levels most often used for housing and other nonretail functions.

Organizing Structure

A grid street system, involving the simplest approach to surveying, subdividing, and selling land, created a well-defined, organized, and understandable spatial structure for the cities' architecture and overall development. Because the street provided the main access to the consumer market, competition for street

Only a few cities had plans that reserved a block for a town square or an outdoor market, making significant open space rare at the core of the typical city center. Occasionally, modifications to the street grid would create unbuildable lots and, thus, unplanned open spaces. The scarcity of open space gave it special value, increasing its impact as a counterpoint and contrast to the architecture of the city.

Residential streets and neighborhood parks designed and developed by city planner Alexander Shepherd provided early residents of Washington with a high-quality street network and public realm.

12

The F Street retail district had become the dominant commercial area in the Washington region by the 1940s. People living throughout the city were able to use the excellent trolley service to reach the stores, theaters, and restaurants in the heart of the city.

Changes in the City Center's Market Composition

During the 20th century, changes in transportation, land use, economics, and demographics had dramatic effects on city centers. Although complex cause-and-effect relationships underlie these changes, it is possible to highlight a number of reasons why city centers faltered and declined.

Toward the end of the 19th century, the emergence of horse-drawn carriages and electric streetcars allowed places for work, home, and leisure to become separate and to disperse. By the 1950s, the automobile further enhanced the mobility of city residents and businesses. Truck transport became cheaper and more convenient, freeing many businesses from the need to be located adjacent to rivers or railroads. As the population and the economy expanded, the move out of the central area accelerated.

An early sign of city center decline was the loss of many of the more affluent residents. As the city center expanded, profitable business uses encroached on neigh-borhoods, reducing the quality of the living environment. As the housing stock in these residential areas aged and their attractiveness declined, those who could afford to do so moved out of the city center and commuted to work.

New technologies allowed high-rise construction, which drove up city center land values and made small-scale residential neighborhoods difficult to sustain. This loss marked the city center's transformation from a diversified market, with an extended day and night cycle of activity, to a more specialized, limited-use business district dependent on daytime activities.

By the mid-1950s, access to the Washington city center had become more difficult because the trolley network was eliminated to provide additional street right-of-way for automobile, truck, and bus traffic. Parking problems also emerged due to the scarcity of off-street parking facilities.

The White House gardens and Lafayette Park are the most important public spaces in Washington. The tree-lined boulevard extending north from Lafayette Park has provided the positive environmental framework for reinvestment and development of this historic corridor.

Changes in the City Center's Physical Character

With the loss of retail and residential uses, as well as a significant amount of employment, many cities were left with specialized facilities such as hospitals, court buildings, professional offices providing legal and financial services, and government, cultural, and educational facilities.

The life cycle of the city declined as only those uses that could be supported by daytime use became viable. Storefront vacancies became more common as higher-end tenants left the center city and were never replaced. This left only marginal businesses that had less ability to invest in building maintenance, which resulted in a further cycle of decline and disinvestment in the city center's economic base.

Lafayette Park and other important public spaces in Washington were the focus of public and private investment when retail and residential uses relocated to sites outside the city center. New office and service commercial activities were developed around each of the historic green spaces to spark the city's economic regeneration.

The great streets and boulevards of Washington provide the unifying physical framework for new investment and a high-quality environment for pedestrian activities and special events. The public realms on K Street (left) and Pennsylvania Avenue (below) were redesigned and rebuilt to encourage greater public use of these important civic spaces.

Changing Values and Attitudes

Although many cities have experienced decline over the past 50 years, an enormous market exists today for the well-planned city. This is due to a change in values and a new appreciation of urban life and the environment, as well as improved management and design of the city center. City centers are taking advantage of their competitive position created by the number and variety of activities that they offer. In addition to providing permanent locations for offices, headquarters, and distribution centers, city centers can meet the demand for cultural facilities, sporting venues, meeting places, and lodging. These facilities and activities bring together business interests, consumers, and all the dynamic support systems required by modern commerce. As the city centers express their individuality and capitalize on their strengths, they provide a rich and rewarding quality of life.

15

A world that can be modified progressively against a background of valued remains, is a world in which one can leave a personal mark alongside the marks of history.

—Kevin Lynch

CHAPTER 2

Regeneration Principles

Seven basic principles for successful urban regeneration can be extracted from initiatives of the past 20 years. These principles are the following:

* ❖ Promote diversity of use.
* ❖ Encourage compactness.
* ❖ Foster intensity of development.
* ❖ Ensure a balance of activities.
* ❖ Provide for accessibility.
* ❖ Create functional linkages.
* ❖ Build a positive identity.

Principle 1: Promote Diversity of Use

A healthy city center should have a wide mix of uses that function in a mutually supportive fashion to establish a diverse and lively business and leisure environment. By offering people a wide variety of reasons to visit and to stay in the heart of the city throughout the day and evening, cities can attract more people more frequently and for a longer period of time. The mix of uses should include office, residential, and entertainment, as well as retail and restaurants.

State Street, Chicago.

by foot. A major priority is to fill the existing gaps in the urban fabric, especially at high-visibility locations in the city center's core. Even relatively small gaps in the continuity of buildings can significantly inhibit the flow of pedestrians. If major anchors and activity centers are too far apart, or isolated from one another by surface parking or vacant storefronts, pedestrian activity and economic synergy can be reduced.

Theaters and cultural facilities located in the heart of the retail district create a lively business and leisure environment. Enhancement of the public realm and development of a new outdoor activity space complement the mix of uses in Portland, Oregon.

Moreover, these uses should be linked via public infrastructure. To take maximum advantage of the potential market, it is critical that there be a balance of functions linked by the public infrastructure and by patterns of pedestrian movement.

Principle 2: Encourage Compactness

Many cities are building on underused sites to establish a compact urban core. Preservation of historic buildings adds richness and visual interest to the streets of Washington, D.C., (left) and the parks of Boston (right).

To promote pedestrian activity, the central area of the city must be compact, creating a critical mass of activity easily accessible

In many cities, new higher-density development tends to be located outside the central area where land prices are lower and parcels are more easily assembled. If located within walking distance of the city center's traditional retail center, peripheral higher-density development is not a problem; however, if people cannot walk between the traditional center and the new development, the impact on the core can be negative.

Principle 3: Foster Intensity of Development

While densities are important in fostering critical mass, it is important that new large-scale projects not have a negative impact on the city center's existing assets, building stock, or street-level activity. In smaller cities with lower densities of development, protection of existing investment may be preferable to overly ambitious development projects.

If appropriate codes and guidelines are not in place, zoning that allows high-density development can create pressures to clear away older buildings whose architectural character adds to the quality of the city center. Zoning often permits new construction that is out of scale with the existing pattern of development, opening the door to a discontinuous

pattern of development with mid-rise historic buildings mixed with high-rise towers, suburban-type development, and a sea of surface parking. The city center plan, development regulations, and the review process must specify how buildings should relate to the street and set standards for the quality of street-level spaces. Continuity along the street, with interesting shop windows and entrance lobbies, creates a consistent sense of spatial enclosure along the pedestrian corridor.

Appropriately scaled infill development and the productive use of upper-story building space for offices or housing can significantly increase the mix and efficiency of land use. Placement of taller buildings at the center or rear of a block and stepping the height up gradually to break up the mass of the new structure visually constitutes an effective strategy for intensifying land use without undermining the city's human scale.

Development of a new central open space is important in cities that lack a sense of place in their city center. In Cincinnati, Ohio, a major green space and plaza were created to complement the high-density office development that was occurring in the core area.

The recycling of an old warehouse into an art center in Alexandria, Virginia, attracted people to existing nearby shops and restaurants and created new life and vitality in the evenings and on weekends.

Principle 4: Ensure a Balance of Activities

The city center must have a balance of activity during the day and in the evening. A disproportionate amount of office space, for example, can leave the central area empty after working hours, so efforts should be made to bring the area alive during those periods with a mix of shops, visitor attractions, and housing.

Excessive clustering of major uses should be avoided; creation of special precincts—the hallmark of many "edge city" environments—is likely to waste the opportunity to maximize the contribution those uses could make to the city center's regeneration.

Principle 5: Provide for Accessibility

While vehicular access and parking must be convenient and efficient, it is important to give the pedestrian clear priority in order to encourage walking and enliven the streets. Sufficiently wide walkways and amenities to enhance the pedestrian experience are necessary if streets are to serve as linkages rather than barriers. A well-defined circulation pattern will ensure a high-quality pedestrian environment, efficient vehicular access, and access to mass transit.

Priority should be given to space for short-term, on-street parking to support shopping and convenience services in the central core. Where possible, the increasing

A high-quality pedestrian environment will encourage walking, enhance bus and transit ridership, and make retail streets more inviting for shoppers. North Michigan Avenue in Chicago is one of the most successful pedestrian-oriented streets in the world.

The comprehensive development of the pedestrian network in Portland provides linkages between the retail core, the riverfront, residential neighborhoods, and the many parks and open-space amenities in the city center.

demand for all-day commuter parking in the city center should be reduced through the use of public transit, peripheral parking, and carpools. In larger cities, underground parking is usually required to attract high-quality tenants and residents to high-density office and residential projects.

Principle 6: Create Functional Linkages

People must be able to walk between activity centers using linkages that are direct, physically attractive, and convenient. Pedestrian connections should create an integrated network defined by distinctive streetscape treatments, open spaces, and active street-level uses, tying together city center activity as well as linking the city center with adjacent neighborhoods.

New development should not be permitted if it detracts from the pedestrian experience by interposing blank walls, parking lots, or parking structures that directly front the street. Design guidelines should promote street-level facades that add interest to the pedestrian environment. Throughblock connections between main streets and nearby parking lots should be encouraged, where possible.

Principle 7: Build a Positive Identity

City centers require a positive identity to create a desirable and interesting place for people to interact. Retailing, cultural activities, entertainment, recreation, and special events programming contribute to an image of the city center as an exciting place to be. Housing and the promotion of urban living also are important in shaping the city center's image as a safe, well-maintained, and livable environment. Marketing and promotions, including joint marketing of events, festivals, discounted parking opportunities, and special incentive days, also promote the attributes of the city center.

A special sense of place was created with the development of the plaza and outdoor café at Westlake Center in Seattle, Washington. The positive identity associated with this public space has benefited the multiblock retail and office district surrounding the plaza.

*We must believe, because it is true,
that people are affected by their environment…
by space and scale, color and texture, by nature and beauty,
that they can be uplifted, made comfortable, made important.*

—James Rouse

CHAPTER 3

Market Components

Each major city center component—offices, retail, housing, cultural and entertainment facilities, and hotels and conference/convention centers—is important to the vitality of the city center. This chapter explores the role that each type of use plays, and the factors that influence its development and success in cities.

Offices

City center office developments create jobs, tax revenues, and a critical mass of potential consumers for other uses such as restaurants, shopping, and entertainment. Therefore, they often set the pace for growth of other city center uses.

Office uses frequently perform the strongest and most prevalent economic function in city centers because they typically require a centralized location and access to other business services. They also are the largest users of and demand generators for higher-intensity developments. When kept in scale with the city center's overall physical character, the intensity of use is a positive factor.

Quincy Market, Boston.

North Michigan Avenue in Chicago is a high-density office corridor and successful retail street. The high quality of the office and retail facilities has stimulated major investment in residential and hotel development in the historic districts east and west of the avenue.

While offices are often the largest space user, it still is important to maintain a diversity of uses at the street level to ensure a lively pedestrian environment. Where office demand prices out other functions, incentives such as density bonuses are needed to encourage retail and residential uses in office developments.

The city center and the suburbs often compete to capture their share of the regional office market. The potential demand for office space is subject to a range of variables such as distance from a competing city or regional hub, density of the city, presence of special nodes of activity (i.e., the state capital, a sports venue, or a major university), and the economic growth of the region.

In smaller cities, office demand to a large extent stems from professional service providers, such as financial institutions, insurance companies, accountants, lawyers, and health care professionals. When the market is weak, incentives can be used to encourage speculative office development, which can then attract new tenants. The public sector can support the market by concentrating government functions in the city center, as well as by providing shared parking and other public amenities.

The office and financial district in Boston has grown and prospered with the creation of Post Office Square, a public park in the historic heart of the city (left). Smaller cities like Alexandria, Virginia, have attracted office developers by constructing a high-quality streetscape and public realm (right).

24

Local financial institutions can be important partners in office projects because they often desire high-visibility, high-quality, mixed-use developments, and often are prepared to take the lead. They also can provide financing and equity for other developments and can inspire additional capital investment in the heart of the city center.

Because the potential for office development is limited in smaller cities, other economic activities are needed to support local retail businesses, hotels, and service providers. In these cities, housing and cultural/entertainment uses will become important activity generators in the overall development strategy.

Retail

While retail use is not the main contributor to city center property values or investment, it is usually important to the vitality and image of the city. Retail is also a visible indicator of economic health, typified by a vibrant street life, in contrast to the negative image created by vacant storefronts. It is the quality and variety of the retail mix, not simply the total square footage, that is the key measure of a vibrant retail sector.

City centers will not only offer a mixture of convenience, service commercial, and specialty retail, but also will need to offer it within a high-quality environment to create a distinctive market identity. An attractive outdoor environment—a plaza, a special street, or a waterfront—can contribute substantially to this image. Such space serves as a social gathering point

and as an identifying element to help reinforce existing businesses and to draw new investment into the central area.

Retail development is usually not the first step in city center renewal; rather, retail usually follows successful development of office and/or residential uses that create a market to support retail functions. New cultural, entertainment, and recreational uses also can help support new retail space.

Forms of Retail Development

City center retail developments can take many forms. Among them are the regional centers, specialty marketplaces, mixed-use projects, outdoor markets and street vendors, and neighborhood service retail.

In Denver, Colorado, the 13-block transit mall was constructed to improve access to the office and retail center of the city. The pedestrian environment is attractive, but the elimination of automobile traffic limits the opportunity to bring high-quality retail stores back to this important image street.

The most successful retail streets in the world provide both a high-quality pedestrian environment and automobile access to the retail frontage. Visibility and accessibility are critical to the development of a healthy retail district.

The Pioneer Place retail center in Portland, Oregon, was designed to reinforce street activity (above). Many large-scale projects have failed because their retail space was oriented internally rather than to the street.

Specialty markets have succeeded in large regional areas like Boston and London. Quincy Market in Boston (below) and Covent Garden in London (bottom) are exciting places to visit because of the pubs, restaurants, entertainment, and specialty retail they offer.

Regional Centers. These typically are anchored by one or more department stores and are likely to contain a large proportion of national chain stores. Most cities with successful regional centers already have a base of department stores. Because large retailers normally are cautious about opening new stores, it can be difficult to develop a regional center in a city center if anchor stores originally located there have already left or if new anchors have not signed on as part of the development plan.

One weakness inherent in regional centers is that they contain a predominance of chain stores, which do not offer a substantially different shopping experience from that found in centers outside the core area. Also, if the regional center is not made part of the traditional core, it can siphon off shoppers from the central area's existing retail businesses. Therefore, a city center regional center needs to be designed carefully to avoid creation of an insular, internally oriented development that turns its back on the city.

Specialty Marketplaces. These developments are anchored by food and entertainment uses rather than by traditional department stores. A large proportion of their total floor area—30 to 50 percent—typically is devoted to restaurants and fast-food vendors catering to lunchtime office workers, tourists, and weekend and evening entertainment patrons. To be successful, these centers must have ready access to multiple markets and a large trade area population. Usually this type of retail center also contains smaller boutiques and specialty shops

for books, music, arts, and home furnishings and is owned by individual entrepreneurs.

Specialty marketplaces typically benefit from a prime location and/or a unique environment such as a waterfront or a historic district. Faneuil Hall in Boston is an example of how a mix of specialty retail and entertainment at a high-quality physical setting creates a vibrant specialty marketplace. It is also an example of a place where substantial public investment was required to establish an attractive public environment with appropriate infrastructure and parking.

Mixed-Use Projects. Anchored by office, residential, hotel, and/or cultural uses, these developments often incorporate retail uses into the first level of their buildings. The benefit of this approach is that it creates a built-in market for retail and an ability to allocate total building and amenity costs over the larger floor area of the building.

Baltimore, Maryland's Inner Harbor area is an excellent example of mixed-use development, integrating regional attractions with retail shops and restaurants to energize the waterfront. Successful development of the Inner Harbor has helped boost development of new office buildings, hotels, and residential dwellings in the city center.

Cities of all sizes have discovered the need to activate public spaces with outdoor markets and street vendors. The market in Munich, Germany, draws people to the city from throughout the region.

Outdoor Markets and Street Vendors.

These features can create interest along city streets and attract consumers with relatively low purchasing power. Special farmers and artisans markets and related activities can attract visitors to city center parking lots on weekends when they normally would be underused.

Neighborhood Service Retail. This typically includes such uses as groceries, drugstores, delicatessens, dry cleaners, and beauty salons that serve the immediate area. These uses help to support a market for city center residential development. In higher-income neighborhoods, specialty marketplaces also can provide a mixture of specialty retail, restaurants, and entertainment uses.

Retail Market Assessment

Potential retail demand depends on the local market context and the regional trade area. As part of developing a strategy for retail regeneration, an objective analysis of market potential can be prepared that will inform planners and developers of the type and magnitude of retail development that can be supported. Market research for retail projects typically involves two types of analysis:

❖ *Economic research.* A quantitative, detailed definition of the trade area and an overview of economic conditions, economic research focuses on employment trends and projections by sector, population growth, household income, disposable income, and retail sales. It also includes an evaluation of competitive retail centers within the trade area. Through analysis of this information, projections can be made of the city center's potential retail sales capture rate and overall retail demand.

❖ *Consumer market research.* This provides qualitative information on the trade area's potential consumers and their shopping preferences and patterns. Consumer research may include telephone interviews of sample households; random, on-site interviews of people on the street; and focus groups—discussions with small groups of consumers to determine attitudes, opinions, and spending habits.

Once the city's retail market is identified, a retail development program can be established and implemented using the following guidelines:

❖ *Maximize visibility and accessibility.* It is important to provide excellent pedestrian circulation and continuity from one block to another.

❖ *Recognize the importance of ground-level retail links to cultural, conference, hotel, and office activities.* It is important to identify potential linkages, high-traffic pedestrian routes, and through-block connections between parking areas and the principal retail street frontage.

❖ *Maximize retail opportunities within mixed-use developments.* Retail uses can be subsidized by office or residential uses and can provide lively streetfronts and linkages to the busiest pedestrian thoroughfares.

❖ *Identify where public sector involvement and financial support is required.* This assistance can take many forms—funds for testing market potential and preparing development concepts, land assembly and writedown, or the development of parking structures and improvements to the public environment.

❖ *Emphasize eating and drinking establishments.* Restaurants and bars serve as focal points for daytime and evening activity.

❖ *In smaller cities, focus retail in a single location.* This will discourage formation of separate retail concentrations that compete with one another. Also, creation of a critical mass of activity will help to increase the drawing power of the central area retail sector.

Design and development of walkways 20 to 30 feet (six to nine meters) wide encourage property owners and merchants to activate their frontage and enliven the street experience. An outdoor café on North Michigan Avenue in Chicago (top) and a neighborhood retail street in Portland (above) illustrate how wider walkways provide space for public amenities.

Cities often use areas in public parks and plazas to provide space for outdoor dining. A portion of the 16th Street right-of-way in Denver has been used to increase the seating capacity of restaurants that face the street.

29

❖ *Develop interesting public space that has a strong local identity and that encourages pedestrian activity.* Retail regeneration will be enhanced by improvement of the public realm and by effective management of circulation, transit, and parking.

❖ *Protect existing shops from new retail competition.* This conflict can be diminished by providing links between new and existing retail activities or by bringing established merchants into new retail spaces to complement the product mix and help provide critical mass.

❖ *Develop a comprehensive approach to merchandising, marketing, and promotion.* The merchandise mix may need to be reoriented from the traditional concentration of convenience, service, restaurant, and specialty retail uses. Existing retail floor plans may need to be reconfigured to accommodate more contemporary merchandising.

Housing

Housing is important to the city center's vitality because local residents extend the level of activity, as well as provide a market for a variety of uses and a group to lobby for high-quality public services and infrastructure. The availability of city center housing is expanding, with the growth being generated by:

❖ changing demographics, including increasing numbers of households made up of young professionals and empty nesters;

❖ a revived interest in urban lifestyles and historic architecture, combined with opportunities in the city center for imaginative and reasonably priced housing in buildings converted from other uses (i.e., warehouses and older office buildings);

❖ a growing white-collar workforce;

The marina and waterfront amenities on Granville Island in Vancouver, Canada, provide an ideal setting for residential development. A park and greenway system allows pedestrian access to the historic retail market on the island. Developers of city center housing prefer to design and build projects that are near public amenities and commercial services.

❖ concentrated cultural and entertainment activities in the center city;

❖ easy access to work and other activities offered by the city center; and

❖ advantages of reverse commuting.

While there has been a sharp rise in the demand for city center housing, disincentives and barriers to new residential development remain, including:

❖ difficulty in assembling sites;

❖ relatively high land costs;

❖ dependence on public financial assistance to develop market-rate housing;

❖ greater market risk, especially in the pioneering stage;

❖ negative perceptions about crime, congestion, and parking;

❖ potential displacement of existing lower-income inner-city residents;

❖ restrictive and antiquated fire, safety, zoning, and building codes; and

❖ noise, trash, and quality-of-life issues.

To establish the central area as a vital, interesting place to live, several initiatives need to be tackled simultaneously. Initial housing developments should be concentrated in areas close to the city center or centers of activity. Scattered projects that lack neighborhood ambience will fail to do this effectively.

The public sector needs to be proactive in developing city center housing. Where the office market is strong and out-competes residential uses for prime city center locations, economic incentives or zoning requirements may be needed to introduce residential uses as part of mixed-use developments. This mixing of housing with other viable uses can improve the financial feasibility and cash flow of the overall project. In the early stages, public incentives and financial assistance that reduce development costs are often vital. Such strategies include: land assembly and writedown, revenue bond financing and low-interest loans, tax abatement, brownfield mitigation, and improvement of streetscapes, parks, parking, and infrastructure. Zoning and building codes often need to be modified to encourage central area housing and to permit conversion of older commercial structures to residential use.

Small courtyards are an important amenity in many urban areas; larger green spaces are also needed to provide space for active and passive recreation. Chicago (left) and San Francisco (right) have developed outstanding residential projects that demonstrate how well-designed high-density housing can be integrated into the fabric of the city.

The historic buildings in the Warehouse District of Cleveland, Ohio, have been renovated for residential and commercial use, providing housing for more than 3,000 people. Street-level shops and restaurants have brought life and vitality to the entire central area of the city.

Smaller historic towns like Alexandria have established architectural guidelines to preserve and enhance private property values in existing urban neighborhoods. Infill development of low-density attached housing can also stimulate private investment in adjacent retail districts.

The following guidelines can be useful in creating city center neighborhoods:

❖ *Concentrate energy and resources on one area at a time.* Focus first on areas that already have marketable assets, such as an established core of residential use or a distinctive architectural or urban design character and scale.

❖ *Capitalize on the special draw of a waterfront, park, or other urban amenities.* Where such an amenity does not exist, it is often possible to create a unique asset, such as a park, square, or other public feature.

❖ *Encourage design solutions that provide residential frontage on the street.* Provide secure, resident-oriented common areas on the street frontage or in the interior of the development.

❖ *Encourage a variety of housing types and price ranges.* Strive for a balance among market-rate and subsidized units, rental and owner-occupied units, and high-rise, mid-rise and low-rise units, while targeting a significant proportion of units to middle-income households as the largest potential market segment.

❖ *Establish development guidelines to encourage property owners to upgrade neighborhoods.* Architectural controls for renovation and new construction can help protect the area's architectural character as well as raise property values. Encouraging the conversion of older, large structures into professional offices, restaurants, boutiques, and single- and multifamily residences can help build the fabric and economic health of a neighborhood.

Cultural and entertainment facilities often thrive in historic districts that have been restored and revitalized. The Pioneer Square historic area in Seattle, Washington, provides an ideal setting for art galleries, antique shops, museums, and restaurants.

Cultural and Entertainment Facilities

Cultural and entertainment facilities help to establish the city center as a leisure and visitor destination and to enhance a city's self-image and quality of life. These attractions can include refurbished historic theaters; centers for the performing arts; sports venues; studios and galleries; history, fine arts, and science museums; and outdoor entertainment spaces. These amenities provide a market for business and convention trade and increased leisure activity. Special events and other promotions increase the number of city center users and the amount of consumer expenditures, as well as improve the city center's appeal as an environment in which to live and work.

To unlock the development potential for cultural and entertainment facilities, they should be integrated into the fabric of the city center. The public sector should prepare a conceptual development plan for a cultural district to ensure the optimal density, mix, and configuration of development. This plan should identify development opportunities, set standards to ensure high-quality development, and establish guidelines for the protection and rehabilitation of important structures.

The new city center park in Tacoma, Washington, was designed and developed to provide an outdoor activity space for the restored civic theater. To be successful, cultural and entertainment districts need to have thoughtfully designed and programmed community event space.

33

Hotels and Conference/Convention Centers

Modern hotels and meeting facilities provide accommodations for visitors as well as opportunities for the local and regional population. Unfortunately, cities have seen hotels and motels proliferate on the periphery of the urban core, along major highways, and adjacent to airports. To attract major hotels back to the central core, some cities have subsidized site acquisition and development or have assembled incentive packages to attract key hotel operators.

While convention centers have grown in number and popularity over the past three decades, they can be one of the most challenging types of development for small cities. Although convention centers are seen as catalysts for developing visitor business and for creating the synergy that supports hotels, retailers, and services,

sometimes conflict arises because nearby hotels cannot always provide the hotel space the convention center needs to accommodate attendees and delegates. Furthermore, unlike hotels, convention centers have downtime for part of each

Many hotels provide conference and meeting room space for local and regional organizations. The high quality of the interior and exterior public space contributes to the successful marketing of meeting facilities in this city center hotel in Cologne, Germany.

year due to holidays, fluctuations in seasonal use, and required set-up time.

Where location and attractiveness combine with abundant hotel accommodations, a central conference center can be a major stimulus for a city. A conference center should offer meeting space, adjacent accommodations, and a full range of support services, such as restaurants, shopping, and computers and business services, plus exercise and recreational facilities.

Before considering the development of a conference center, a city should explore carefully the prospective markets and examine the project's feasibility. It is possible that existing hotels can expand to include additional conference facilities and that new hotels can be planned to include conference space as part of their total offering—at a size appropriate to support the potential demand for such facilities.

Smaller cities often provide conference and meeting room space in multipurpose facilities that serve many community functions. In Baden Baden, Germany, the park and open-space amenities available in the heart of the city complement the public meeting place.

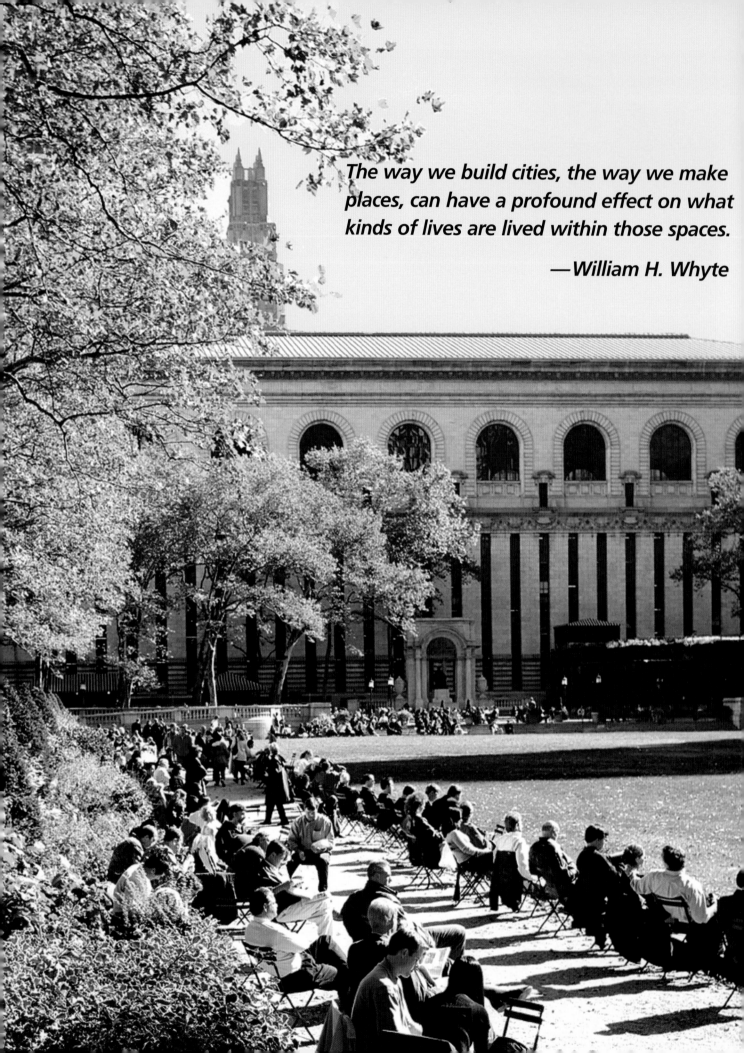

The way we build cities, the way we make places, can have a profound effect on what kinds of lives are lived within those spaces.

—William H. Whyte

Importance of Place

Streets, walkway paving, buildings, and open spaces shape the city center's urban design structure and image as a unique place. Many other design elements—streetlights, paving, plantings, signs— complement this basic structure and contribute to the quality of the city center environment. The overall form, appearance, and arrangement of these diverse elements must be organized to convey a unified image, a sense of vitality, and a comfortable and inviting setting for human activity.

The Relationship between Market and Place

The city center's character as a place plays a key role in whether it succeeds as a market. City center design must encourage pedestrian movement, accommodate special activities, and promote social interaction. The more oriented toward people its environment is, the more the city center will become an attractive focus for investments in new development and renovation. How well its spaces and activities create a smoothly functioning whole will determine whether people will visit, shop at, or work in the city center, and whether they will keep coming back.

Bryant Park, New York City.

The public realm in Portland, Oregon, was designed to encourage pedestrian movement, accommodate special activities, and promote social interaction. Enhancement of the streets has created a positive environment for economic development in the city center and the region.

expression of the city center's economic health and its progress toward regeneration, improvements in the physical setting can help to attract potential users and new residents, creating opportunities for new investment. An improved streetscape, better access via car or transit, more convenient parking, or a public plaza that serves as a focal point and an amenity can help to reawaken private investment in the central area.

The city center's physical environment must welcome people and enhance their experiences. If it does, it will serve as a catalyst for creating a multiple-use market that supports an expanding range of economic and institutional functions.

Place as a Catalyst

Public realm improvements dramatically influence people's perceptions and attitudes toward the heart of the city. Because the physical environment is a visible

By demonstrating the community's commitment to its city center, money spent to improve the quality of the public realm communicates the desire to encourage and protect private investment and to stimulate creative development. Such improvements also can have a direct impact on leveraging private investment by closing the gap between development costs and profitability.

Portland's Pioneer Courthouse Square, a special public place for outdoor activities and events, has been the major catalyst for retail development in the area.

Place as a Market Facilitator

To support a compact development pattern with a critical mass of complementary activities, coordinated planning of pedestrian, transit, and parking systems must take place. Such functional integration promotes market synergy among the city center's mix of uses.

A high-quality pedestrian environment provides a positive setting for leisure activities and encourages the development of desirable central functions, especially housing, retail, and entertainment. Properly designed city center streets, public spaces, and buildings can foster intensive pedestrian use and encourage the active street life that is essential to retail success. Planning and design approaches that encourage people to move through the central area on foot will enable retail and entertainment uses to capitalize on resident populations and employees of local businesses, as well as city center visitors.

This market capture occurs through provision of well-defined connections between anchor uses, creation of streetscapes that establish visual continuity and physical comfort, provision of interest and a sense of human scale at the street level, and establishment of opportunities for special events programming.

Removal of a riverfront highway in Portland opened up land for development of a riverfront promenade and park, and enabled development of the River Place residential area, including convenience stores.

Streetscape improvements in Portland provide visual continuity and physical comfort for retail customers, with sculpture, art, and seasonal plantings adding color and life to the street environment.

39

*The private invest-
ment in Portland that
has accrued since the
late 1970s is directly
linked to the parks
and parkways that
have been built.*

Place as a Sustaining Force

The city center will remain a competitive location for private investment only if new development projects are carefully planned and designed to add to the overall quality of the public realm. If new developments fail to complement (or, in fact, diminish) existing assets or public sector improvements, success in attracting new private investment and broadening the base of central area activity can be limited and short lived.

Unfortunately, many regeneration programs concentrate on strategies for stimulating private investment without determining the best locations for new investments and how they should be designed to enhance the characteristics that make the city center a special place. Quality is as important as quantity: while the volume and dollar value of new construction are easily quantifiable measures of city center economic health, focusing on these numbers can distort an understanding of the factors that underlie successful, long-term regeneration.

It is how well new development is executed and its impact on the quality of the public realm that will determine the real value of the public and private investments in the city center. If the money invested in bricks and mortar fails to enhance the city center's physical structure, its visual appeal, its sense of identity, and its quality as a setting for pedestrian activity, these investments will not build a lasting foundation for economic regeneration.

A Coordinated Approach: Cooperation and Partnership

Careful coordination of the decisions that shape the city center's physical character is required to introduce coherence, promote vitality, enhance comfort, add convenience, and create a distinctive image. To achieve these objectives, there must be a clearly articulated strategy for coordinating decisions made for separate purposes over a long period.

Property owners surrounding New York City's Bryant Park are responsible for the management and maintenance of this six-acre urban site.

The decisions that numerous individual property owners make regarding such issues as maintenance and reuse versus new development influence the character of the city center as a whole. In turn, the character of the whole influences the success of each individual initiative.

Consequently, individual property owners and the public sector must work together to create a successful city center.

Both the public and private sectors need a clear vision of what the city center's physical environment can be—a vision that must stem from a clear understanding of existing assets, definition of and consensus on priorities, and familiarity with what other cities have done in similar situations. Physical improvements, made in the public interest, expand the tax base, increase economic stability, and boost civic pride. Investment in such improvements, therefore, is an appropriate activity for the public sector. However, progress is

more certain when the community at large and private sector decision makers share an understanding of how the urban design objectives maximize the long-term value of investment, and then pursue these objectives through their own internal decision-making processes.

Dense shade trees in Bryant Park frame the central grass panel and provide an ideal place to sit in filtered sun. A gravel walk on the outer edge of the lawn allows people to sit in the sun on movable chairs.

The successful regeneration of Bryant Park provides an excellent example of how to build on existing assets. Bryant Park's movable café chairs are easily rearranged for special events staged on the fountain plaza.

The Framework for Defining Objectives

To define an effective vision, two underlying premises are important.

❖ *Build on existing assets.* Regeneration programs are most effective when they build on the city center's existing physical assets and special visual qualities. Each city center offers a unique foundation on which to build, and it is these local characteristics that should steer the community's approach to defining and strengthening the city center's quality as a place and its vitality as a multiple-use market.

❖ *Take care of the pedestrian.* The quality of the pedestrian experience should be the principal concern in center city urban design. Strategies for humanizing the urban environment and providing a pleasant, diverse, and interesting walking experience should receive the

highest priority. Water features, sculpture, cafés, and entertainers can enliven the pedestrian experience.

Building on Local Assets

The geographic setting, the historic pattern of development, key landmarks, and the architectural heritage make each city center unique and offer opportunities for creating an intelligible structure and a distinctive identity. Each community needs to recognize the physical assets that already benefit its central area and to appreciate how these assets can be the starting points for planning, designing, and coordinating future growth and change.

The importance of building on existing assets should be self-evident. Nevertheless, many early urban regeneration efforts erased the historic fabric of the built environment to promote bigger buildings and what were considered more efficient patterns of circulation. From these efforts, three important lessons emerged:

In Boston, a water feature in Copley Square was designed to provide people with a comfortable place to enjoy the park environs. Redesign and reconstruction of Copley Square has contributed to the economic regeneration of the city's historic Back Bay area.

❖ The human and financial costs of creating a clean slate for new large-scale redevelopment can be unacceptably high.

❖ Suburban development models with their emphasis on the needs of automobiles can destroy the character of the city center's pedestrian environment.

❖ The central area's traditional pattern and scale of development, its architecture, and its history have value and meaning for people.

The central park green in Copley Square provides a broad open space and a prominent setting for outdoor concerts and festivals. A wide, brick-paved promenade offers space for the display and sale of crafts and fresh produce. Initially, the central space was recessed below the elevation of the street and adjoining walkways.

The quality of the pedestrian experience often can be measured by the number of people who use a park or plaza on a nice day. Toronto-Dominion Centre plaza in Toronto, Canada, attracts many people because the paved area and seating are enhanced by the lawn, which adds richness, color, and texture to the space.

Quality of the Pedestrian Experience

To be successful as a market, the city center must be successful as a place for people. Although an exciting skyline, good vehicular or transit access, and convenient parking are all valuable assets, it is the quality of the experience of walking through the city center that is the measure of its success as a place. Certainly, the central area should offer easy, convenient, and continuous pedestrian access among places for shopping, employment, housing, and recreation. It also must establish a high level of amenities and a physical expression of concern for the quality of life, human scale, and physical and psychological comfort and safety.

To provide opportunities for social interaction as well as for observing the life of the city, the design of the central core must encourage activity on the street and in a variety of other public spaces. The city center should present the possibility of choice, surprise, and adventure. Its physical structure should help orient first-time users, while also serving its everyday constituents—local residents, the central area workforce, shoppers, and users of its specialized services. Its visual character must be sufficiently dynamic and complex to remain interesting visit after visit.

Cities that have retained, at least in part, the development pattern and scale of the traditional central area marketplace can offer a satisfying pedestrian experience, and reinforcement or restoration of that fabric can help to create a unique and competitive location for a range of economic functions. An appropriate balance between vehicular and pedestrian needs, a suitable relationship between high-rise buildings and the street, and a positive

Building setbacks of 25 to 30 feet (7.5 to nine meters) and wide walkways, as found on a number of streets in Boston's Back Bay neighborhood, create space for outdoor cafés, special storefront design, and unique signage.

Design and development of pedestrian-oriented space—parks, plazas, and promenades—are essential to achieving a better environment. Cities like Baltimore, Maryland, have committed acres of land to pedestrian circulation, active and passive recreation, and related uses that can activate public space.

level of pedestrian amenities should be achieved with an eye to the traditions of the historic city center marketplace.

Balancing Pedestrian and Vehicular Requirements. Auto access and parking are critical to the city center's success as a market. Nevertheless, a planning approach that consistently gives priority to efficient traffic flows and inexpensive surface parking for individual developments will lower the quality of the pedestrian environment.

All central area streets should be designed with the pedestrian in mind, and on key retail streets, the pedestrian should receive top priority. While vehicular traffic and on-street parking should not be excluded, cars and parking should be carefully managed to avoid overwhelming the human scale of the streets. Parking lots, large parking structures, or overly wide streets must not create gaps or barriers between activity anchors or an unsafe, unpleasant environment for pedestrians.

Pedestrian crosswalks should be designed to encourage people to cross major arterial streets to reach important city center amenities. Access to the waterfront in Baltimore was considered a problem until the city created a wide crosswalk that allowed people to feel safe crossing a high-volume traffic artery.

The area north of the Baltimore Inner Harbor has accommodated high-rise development without harming the public realm around the harbor. Only one office tower was permitted in the waterfront district, while the retail and restaurant pavilions, the National Aquarium, and the Maryland Science Center were required to design low-rise structures to preserve the view corridors to the harbor.

Large-Scale Development. Almost every city center must decide whether and how to accommodate high-rise buildings and other large-scale structures. These buildings can create new landmarks in the cityscape, but they also can bring problems in terms of access and parking requirements. Sensitive transitions in scale can fit these structures into an environment of buildings with lower heights and narrower street frontages.

The promenade around the Inner Harbor allows pedestrians to enjoy walking and provides a place for people to meet and share in the area's activity. The parks and open space along the promenade permit views of the city skyline to the north and the historic landscape to the south.

Most important, such large-scale developments must relate positively to the street at ground level by adding pedestrian amenities. Blank walls, parked vehicles, building vents, and loading areas should be avoided.

Amenities. With the high quality of pedestrian amenities, the interior design of the suburban shopping mall provides lessons about the quality, comfort, and convenience pedestrians expect. These lessons include the consistent use of high-quality materials, creation of focal points and ample seating in inviting social spaces, and the provision of a consistently high level of maintenance.

The city center's specific assets provide it with opportunities to nurture a unique urban ambience and an experience that could never be duplicated at a shopping mall. The central area should be a point of confluence for all social and economic forces within the regional community. With public and private commitment, the city center can become the place where different values and ideas meet and where a broad cross section of residents and visitors rub shoulders. As a result, the city

The activity, color, level of human interaction, and excitement of New York City's Rockefeller Center plaza make it a place people enjoy visiting year-round. This energy and vitality flow to the multiblock retail, office, and entertainment district in midtown Manhattan.

center environment can be heterogeneous, its variety of activities, people, and lifestyles creating surprise and excitement.

Compared with the more controlled and defined environment of a typical suburban shopping mall, the city center will always be set apart by its richer social and cultural textures, its broader range of consumer choices, and its perpetually dynamic quality.

Cities with great places and a high-quality public realm draw millions of visitors and tourists each year. London, Paris, Rome, Venice, New York City, Washington, and Chicago offer special places and spaces that people enjoy visiting. The life and vitality that evolves from the creation of a high-quality public realm is essential to the development and sustainability of every city center.

The outdoor ice rink at Rockefeller Center plaza is popular because of its location in the heart of midtown Manhattan and because the rink is protected from the winter wind. The restaurants and food court at the rink level bring additional ambience and activity to this special place.

The measure of any great civilization is in its cities, and the measure of a city's greatness is to be found in the quality of its public spaces, its parks and squares.

Place Principles

There are seven general principles for making a city center a successful place. They should guide the decisions that shape the city center's evolving form and character as a high-quality place for people and be used as the basis for evaluating each city center's existing assets. These principles are:

- ❖ Create an organizing structure.
- ❖ Foster a distinctive identity.
- ❖ Encourage variety and interest.
- ❖ Ensure visual and functional continuity.
- ❖ Maximize convenience.
- ❖ Provide for comfort.
- ❖ Emphasize high quality.

Principle 1: Create an Organizing Structure

A clear and simple development pattern within the city center enables residents and visitors to understand how the area is organized and to make their way around the city. This organizing structure is crucial to building an identity and a special sense of place in the heart of the city.

Leicester Square, London.

New York City's Fifth Avenue is recognized for its high-quality retail stores, high-density office development, and landmark structures like St. Patrick's Cathedral, but the high-speed, one-way traffic that flows through this important area harms the pedestrian environment.

An intelligible development structure helps people to locate and identify central area uses and activities easily. A city that makes it simple for users to find their way increases the city center's accessibility, both physically and psychologically, and engenders feelings of emotional security, well-being, and competence.

Kevin Lynch's research (*The Image of the City*, 1960) describing how people "read" the urban environment and fit its parts into a coherent pattern provides a strong empirical base for effective urban design decision making. Lynch's theories concerning paths, edges, districts, nodes, and landmarks remain significant and useful today. Strong visual cues reinforce and reveal the functional organization of the city center and enhance the users' experiences there. Major public spaces or landmarks should mark crossroads at the heart of the city center; broad boulevards can define principal paths of movement; and reduced spacing between buildings

and increased building heights should give an accurate visual cue to the location of the central core. In these ways, easily perceived connections are forged between the central area's physical structure and the human purposes it is meant to serve. By making the functional organization of the city more visible, thoughtful urban design enhances the city center's efficient operation and makes it a more meaningful place for people.

It is elements of the city center's public environment that are most influential in creating a clear organizing structure. These elements—the basic street pattern, the roles of streets within the circulation hierarchy, streetscape treatments, and the location and character of the open spaces—all can be managed through public policy and investment decisions to create a powerful urban design framework that gives the city structure, continuity, and coherence.

The Street and Block Pattern

The most basic element of the city center's urban design framework is its street system. How well that system creates a predictable and unifying pattern of similarly sized blocks and regularly spaced intersections will determine the strength of the organizing structure for central area development. Block size has an important influence on the scale of buildings: the relatively small block lengths typical of older central areas—200 to 300 feet (60 to 90 meters)—limit the widths of buildings. Small blocks also enhance convenience for pedestrians by making connections to other blocks and subdistricts easily visible and accessible.

The grid street system in New York City and other American cities can be monotonous if the streetscape and walkways are not designed to reflect the street hierarchy. The street width and public realm should be planned to meet the needs and desires of the property owners and merchants.

Although small blocks may not be the most efficient pattern for maximizing traffic flow or minimizing development costs, they relate more positively to the way people experience the city than do superblocks—300 to 600 feet long (90 to 180 meters)—and megastructures. Whenever decision makers consider interrupting the existing street pattern to allow development at a scale larger than that permitted by existing blocks, they should consider carefully whether their decision will weaken an element that is important in defining the city center's structure, scale, and functional integration.

Hierarchy of Streets

The grid street system, a legacy of the traditional pattern of urban development, continues to be the most common street pattern for the city center. It is easily understood, but it can be monotonous if each street looks like all the others. Some sense of hierarchy should emerge from differences in the widths of rights-of-way, and the treatment of the walkways and the streetscape.

Differing roles for streets within the grid system can enhance the city center's visual structure if street functions are reflected in a corresponding hierarchy of streetscape treatments. Well-defined major arterials, transitways, collector roads, and local access streets reduce the potential for conflicts between through-traffic and local traffic and increase circulation efficiency. Such a hierarchy can also reduce traffic volumes and speeds on streets with pedestrian-oriented development.

Building setbacks can provide space for plazas and fountains, and seating where people can enjoy street activity. While design and development of special places along the street can bring visual relief and sunlight to a high-density corridor, if a series of plazas are built next to each other, the visual unity of the street can be impaired.

The entrance court to Rockefeller Center—a midblock linkage to Fifth Avenue that features a linear water element, sculpture, and colorful seasonal plantings—is the most important entrance to this great urban space. Seating along both sides of this landscape amenity invites people to linger and enjoy this place.

Open Spaces

When carefully embedded within the overall pattern of streets and development blocks, open spaces enhance the legibility of the city center's structure by providing highly visible landmarks. Examples include: linear open spaces or boulevards that help define major vehicular and pedestrian corridors, green spaces that mark gateways to the city center, and public parks and major public plazas that identify activity centers. These open spaces establish a common focus around which land uses and development can be organized; they are the anchors that root individual development parcels and create an attractive and coordinated whole.

In the summer, the central plaza in Rockefeller Center provides additional seating for restaurants that operate on the lower level. The colorful canvas canopies and flowers not only create a warm and friendly setting for outdoor dining, but also enhance the view of people looking down on the space from upper-level walkways.

Land Use and Density

The way development relates to the street can reinforce or weaken the clarity with which the city center's inherent structure can be expressed. For example, a clearly defined progression in development scale and density can signal approach and arrival at the heart of the community. In contrast, when the development lining major entrance corridors to the central area is homogeneous in use, scale, and intensity (e.g., strip commercial development), people will be confused about where the central area begins and ends and how it relates to surrounding districts.

Spatial Definition

Within the city center, buildings play a significant role in reinforcing the overall organizational pattern by creating a solid, continuous architectural edge that defines the street space. The three-dimensional framework of buildings and streets is

The architectural quality of buildings and storefronts, combined with streetscape amenities, make the experience of walking in the city center a pleasure. In midtown Manhattan, the major north-south streets invite people to stroll and enjoy the excitement of being in the city.

weakened when vacant lots, surface parking or deep building setbacks create gaps in the streetwall. In contrast, consistent frontyard setbacks and infill development that repairs and reinforces the existing urban fabric help to unify the city center's structure.

Principle 2: Foster a Distinctive Identity

A vivid, recognizable image can identify the city center as a place with personal and communal meaning. When that identity has an appeal, it is a marketing asset for all city center uses.

A city center development pattern, created by a regular grid of streets and blocks and reinforced by buildings that form a continuous, enclosing streetwall, establishes a strong foundation for building such a recognizable image. Through repeated use of minor visual elements, the city center's buildings, streetscapes, and open spaces also can blend multiple layers of detail into consistent themes. These

In older residential areas of Boston, building setbacks provide space for outdoor cafés, courtyards, and gardens. This additional space creates an opportunity to help foster a distinctive identity in the heart of the city.

The historic buildings in Seattle, Washington's Pioneer Square have been restored and renovated for use as restaurants, art galleries, professional offices, and specialty retail and antique shops. The buildings form the walls of this outdoor space, the trees create a roof, and the signs and flowers add color and texture.

thematic continuities can include spatial relationships, architectural forms and details, materials, colors, signs, and street furniture. The choice and layering of thematic elements should be carefully considered, establishing image and orientation but avoiding creation of superfluous detail and features characteristic of Hollywood stage sets. Consistent themes must first be identified, then strategies for reinforcing them and creating unifying characteristics must be implemented.

Where the central area is large enough to contain specialized subdistricts close to an intensive, multiple-use core, each subdistrict should project a distinctive identity. At the same time, individual subdistricts must be recognizable as part of the larger city center area. Some of the design themes that identify the core can extend into each of the subdistricts (e.g., streetlights, street trees, paving materials) with slight variations to mark the character of each subdistrict. Strong, clearly defined, and convenient pedestrian links that tie each subdistrict to the core are also essential.

Historic Buildings

The human scale, high-quality materials, and rich architectural detailing of buildings constructed in the 19th and early 20th centuries are especially powerful identity-building resources in many city centers. Whether as significant landmark buildings or as supporting structures contributing to a recognizable subdistrict character, older buildings add a sense of historic continuity and a link to the community's past achievements.

To capitalize on this asset, those entrusted with the city center's future must aggressively pursue conservation of landmarks, historic buildings, and historic blocks. The renovation and adaptive use of older structures and the restoration of traditional storefronts can bring dramatic improvement to the central area's image. Even modest improvements such as fresh paint or new signs will upgrade the city center's appearance and foster a renewed sense of identity and well-being.

New development should reinforce or complement the positive elements that give existing architecture its interest and character. This is especially true at the street level, where visibility and impact are greatest. The reinforcement of local or regional architecture—instead of the use of anonymous architecture—should be encouraged because such local personality makes it easier to sustain a strong city center image.

Geography

Topography, views, and other natural assets can lend a special identity to the city and its central area. Waterfronts are especially important resources in places where changes in transportation and development economics have made land and buildings available for reuse. When waterfront areas are redeveloped with a variety of attractions, they can change the image of the city center and play a pivotal role in building a positive new identity.

The architecture of infill development in Charleston, South Carolina, has been designed to reflect the historic scale and character of the existing buildings.

Design and development of the riverfront park and promenade in Cologne, Germany, attracted private investment to the banks of the Rhine River, bringing hotels and restaurants overlooking this linear park and changing the city's riverfront image.

Fountain Square in Cincinnati, Ohio, with its fountain and sculpture, has become an icon in the city center. The plaza is the most popular meeting place for people who live and work in the city and serves as an ideal location for special events and festivals.

Landmarks

Landmarks can take many forms, such as a building, an arcade, a public space, a fountain, or a clock. The quality that distinguishes landmarks from other city center features is their ability to stand out from their surroundings, a trait that can be used to orient users and create a sense of identity and civic pride. Especially for out-of-town visitors, landmarks are often the most memorable elements in the cityscape, representing or symbolizing the entire city center. Such landmarks provide an opportunity for a form of "branding," where an icon is instantly imprinted, widely recognized, and associated with positive images. Public improvements as well as carefully planned private development can create new landmarks that reinforce the center's identity.

Buildings that are distinguished from surrounding development by height, mass, architectural style, or richness of detailing can be useful landmarks. However, these elements are most effective when they stand in contrast to a consistent and unified background.

Streetscape Treatments

Because streets act as the foreground for people moving through the city center, the

Streetscape improvements in Portland, Oregon, established a high-quality environment for private investment in the central area. The brick paving and streetscape elements add a richness to the walkways and provide a unifying physical structure for development in the city center.

streetscape has the potential to establish a clear identity for the center through the consistent use of well-designed benches, light standards, street tree plantings, and other streetscape elements. The use of special paving materials also can help to unify the central area by visually bridging streets or changes in land use. All these elements need to be designed and blended into a coherent whole, not installed piecemeal or without regard for their impact on the overall character of the public realm. The key to maximizing the potential of a streetscape is to create a sense of identity consistent with urban design elements found in similar settings in the city center.

Public Art

A strong arts orientation, including the use of sculpture, fountains, and building graphics, can become one of the city center's identifying themes. When carefully designed, even utilitarian components—tree grates, benches, manhole covers, fencing, and signs—can become art elements worthy of attention and admiration. In addition to supporting the identity of the city center, public art helps to humanize the environment. It can introduce a sense of humor or underscore the historic significance of a particular place to engage people's attention and add meaning to the urban experience. Art is used most successfully when it is integrated into the total design for a public space—a plaza, park, or pedestrian walkway.

Public Spaces

A public space located at the city center's crossroads can serve as a significant identity builder. If the space is both a visual

focal point and an important activity center, it becomes a powerful symbol and a place that lives in the visitor's memory as the essence of the city center.

Most city centers lack such a special place, but when one can be created, it is well worth the cost. Size is not the primary prerequisite: to function effectively as an identity element, a central public space should be designed and programmed for maximum visibility and accessibility. It should be adaptable for a wide variety of functions, incorporate actively programmed edges, provide a significant amount and variety of seating, and represent the best possible quality of design and materials.

The contemporary sculpture designed for the entrance plaza at Illinois Center in Chicago provides visual stimulus for people entering office buildings or walking along the east side of North Michigan Avenue. At lunchtime, the sculpture is the focus for people dining or relaxing on the plaza.

The trellis and fountain at Post Office Square in Boston are amenities designed to encourage people to visit the park and enjoy the green space that has been created in the center of the financial district.

Six historic park squares in Savannah, Georgia, were restored to encourage property owners to invest in renovating their private residences, and within three years, many had updated their historic homes. A few years later, additional money was raised from the community to install a fountain and to design related furniture in Orleans Square.

Smaller local parks and plazas also can be identifying elements for the city center's subdistricts. These open spaces should be part of the integrated system of pedestrian linkages, creating a positive visual structure for the central area and a specific local identity for adjacent development.

Principle 3: Encourage Variety and Interest

Just as it provides a range of uses and activities, the city center should be a rich, diverse, and complex environment offering a range of sensory stimuli. As a dynamic place, it should include elements that change frequently enough to keep the city center fresh, interesting, and exciting. Changes can range from new storefront displays to a roster of programmed activities and events.

Although visual variety and complexity evolve naturally in most cities, in some central areas it needs to be cultivated. But the variety should not be chaotic and must not be allowed to diminish the overall visual cohesiveness of the city center. Consequently, it is important to

The outdoor events plaza in Alexandria, Virginia, was designed to accommodate a wide range of community activities. People visiting this historic town center often take time to relax in this civic space.

promote variety in smaller-scale elements —architectural details, banners, and storefronts—that relate to the pedestrian realm. Transparent ground-level facades that share the interior activities with the street, indoor uses that spill outdoors in good weather (produce markets, cafés, street vendors), and special events programming are important elements in promoting variety and interest.

Principle 4: Ensure Visual and Functional Continuity

A unifying visual matrix is needed to allow the viewer to scan the urban scene, rapidly understand the whole, and select particular details of interest. Visual continuity also is crucial to individual merchants whose success depends, at least in part, on the ease with which potential patrons can locate and identify their businesses. If a strong organizing structure is created by a regular street pattern, uniform block sizes, well-located open spaces, and consistent relationships between buildings and the street, it will be easier to achieve visual and functional continuity. But continuity also depends on the careful treatment of other urban design elements.

Many small towns have redesigned and developed the pedestrian realm to provide visual and functional continuity along important streets. In Williamsburg, Virginia, the walks were expanded to provide space for outdoor cafés and special events (above). The narrow walks and streetscape in Southhampton, New York, complement the well-designed storefronts and amenities furnished and maintained by the shop owners (below).

59

Mature street trees and buildings form the vertical walls that define the linear street space. Building architecture visible above the trees forms the structure for the street, but the design of the building facades below the tree canopy establishes the street's quality and image. The street trees in Portland reveal only the upper stories of the buildings (top), while in Seattle, the tree canopy draws attention to the storefronts (above).

Architecture

Although uniform building heights can be a powerful factor in creating a sense of visual continuity, such consistency requires a degree of regulatory oversight that is rarely possible. Nevertheless, careful transitions between buildings of different heights can help to reduce discontinuities.

Continuity at the ground level, where impact on the pedestrian experience is greatest, may be the most important priority. Here, similarities in building materials and in the massing of building form should be encouraged, as should consistent spacing between buildings, positive relationships in the location and proportions of facade openings, and the organi-

zation of the facade into clearly defined base and upper stories. The objective is to coordinate the design of the city center's buildings to make each blockface read as a coherent architectural unit.

Continuity requires compatibility while also allowing for design variation. The basic strategy is to identify characteristic approaches to the use of design elements in creating an architectural composition and to repeat selected design linkages from one building to another. Furthermore, the closer together buildings are clustered, the more important continuity becomes. Similarly, the smaller the city center area and the fewer the buildings, the more important continuity is and the less tolerance there can be for dramatic contrasts in form, materials, massing, and height.

Streetscape

Well-designed streetscapes can be a major factor in creating a sense of identity for the central area and can function as a unifying visual element. Repeated use of a selected vocabulary of street furnishings— light standards, paving, benches, tree plantings, newspaper vending machines, public telephones—creates a visual overlay that reinforces the city center's organizing structure of streets and development blocks.

The planting of street trees is one of the best investments in the public realm a city can make. Especially where upper-story architecture is uninspiring or lacks continuity, a canopy of trees can provide a unifying visual structure while preserving the visibility of storefronts and signs from

the pedestrian walkway and streets. To reinforce the linear character of urban street spaces, street trees should be regularly spaced and located a uniform distance from the curb. Care should be taken in selecting the trees to be planted; sunlight levels, canopy size, and fall color should all be carefully planned and understood.

Streetscape continuity can be achieved over time and at little additional cost through coordination of design guidelines with the city's regular capital program for street improvements. However, a more dramatic short-term improvement may be desirable in selected areas to reinforce or promote private renovation and new development.

Signs

Signs also influence the degree of visual continuity in the city center. Problems with signs that are out of scale, poorly designed, poorly maintained, or simply too numerous can be corrected at a relatively low cost and within a relatively short period to yield dramatic results. Needed are design guidelines to promote consistency in the size, design, and placement of business signs, and a simplified and coordinated program guiding the use and design of public directional and informational signs to organize their presentation and to reduce visual clutter.

Linkages

Links that promote movement among the city center's uses and activities are also crucial in shaping the center's character as a place. Convenient and well-defined connections among office, residential, retail,

entertainment, and cultural uses encourage an extended cycle of intensive pedestrian activity and make it easier for the various uses in the central area to support each other.

Streetscape amenities, colorful awnings, and signage create an inviting environment for shopping in the central area of Princeton, New Jersey. This important retail street benefits from the high-quality stores, storefronts, and historic facades.

Saratoga Springs, New York, in partnership with retail merchants, plants and maintains a flower bed between the walkway and the street (above). Signage and storefront architecture in Saratoga Springs and Alexandria (left) have been designed and implemented based on architectural guidelines and criteria established by the cities.

61

The bus transitway in Denver, Colorado, brings thousands of people into the heart of the city on electric buses that run on an exclusive right-of-way connecting to the rail station, three light-rail lines, and two bus stations serving the city and region. The public space created along the transitway provides room for pedestrians to walk and relax.

Principle 5: Maximize Convenience

Most cities have core areas that can be traversed within ten or 15 minutes. Keeping the city center compact will facilitate access and maximize convenience for users as well as create opportunities for economic interaction among uses.

Pedestrian Movement

One of the highest priorities in creating a physical context that spurs regeneration is to improve the city center as a place for pedestrians. This helps the city center to overcome one of it most difficult challenges: to make the central area an attractive one-stop activity center where a person can make a single vehicle trip, use one parking space, and make multiple stops easily on foot. A compact area, a clear organizational structure, and an integrated system of pedestrian linkages are needed to meet this challenge. In addition, short blocks and through-block accessways make it easier to move between streets; well-defined links between parking resources and retail centers are also important.

Parking

To maximize the city center's convenience and attractiveness as a retail and entertainment location, parking policies should grant priority to short-term users over employees with daily parking needs. Signs helping shoppers to locate parking, as well as parking validation programs that reduce costs to the consumer, can make the central area more competitive with the suburban shopping center. Certainly, an adequate supply of long-term employee parking also must be available; this space can be located farther from workplace destinations—either within a four- to five-block walk or in more remote locations linked to the core by transit shuttles. Enforcement and flexible pricing, based on long- or short-term needs, location, and time of day, are the keys to an effective parking program.

Transit

A transit corridor or loop connecting major activity generators within the city center and linking the core to adjacent districts can provide a convenient alternative to the automobile within the central area. To encourage use of the transit system,

Cities can increase transit ridership by improving the curbside environment where passengers queue up for buses. Denver's transit mall provides comfortable seating areas and amenities that encourage transit patrons to ride the bus.

there should be short headways (intervals) in the service and low or no fares required. Parking supply and pricing that provide a disincentive to making internal trips by car are also important.

Principle 6: Provide for Comfort

Guaranteeing the physical and psychological comfort of pedestrians is paramount. Adequate walkway widths, shade, seating, and a sense of protection from vehic-

ular traffic are essential in creating a comfortable setting for pedestrians; activity, unobstructed visibility, and "eyes on the street" are essential for security. The friendly presence of city center "ambassadors," street vendors, and maintenance workers also can augment psychological comfort.

Four areas of concern in planning for the physical comfort of the central area are climate, traffic, amenities, and physical safety.

Development of streets dedicated exclusively to bus service eliminates the opportunity to accommodate other vehicular traffic. Creation of dedicated bus lanes combined with space allowing limited automobile access is important to retail merchants and restaurant owners who want to provide both a high-quality environment and access to their businesses.

The location of bus shelters can affect pedestrian circulation and retail activity in the immediate area. The large bus shelters in Portland provide protection from inclement weather, but limit visual and physical access to the stores except where they are placed on wide walkways.

Climate

Since climate plays an important role in pedestrian comfort, consideration should be given to siting tall buildings so they do not shade important public spaces, especially during cooler months. Buildings located along streets with an east-west orientation limit sunlight exposure on the south side of the right-of-way. North-south streets provide more continuous sunlight to the street, thus encouraging greater pedestrian activity along important corridors. In warm weather, trees or building-mounted awnings can provide shade, and indoor public gathering places should be developed for use in inclement weather. On buildings more than ten stories tall, use of upper-story setbacks, which reduce wind-tunnel effects on streets and in public spaces, should be encouraged.

Traffic

The design plan for the street should provide an adequate sense of separation and protection between pedestrian areas and vehicular travel lanes. Volume and speed of through-traffic on major pedestrian streets should be controlled to minimize noise and fumes and to enhance pedestrian safety.

Amenities

Amenities such as seating should be located in public spaces and at bus stops for the comfort of transit patrons. Walkways need to be wide enough to accommodate pedestrian through-traffic, window-shopping, bus waiting areas, street trees, and street furniture.

Physical Safety

All paving materials should provide safe walking surfaces and avoid creation of unnecessary changes in elevation that can produce pedestrian hazards. Clearly defined pedestrian street crossings will ensure high visibility and provide a sense of added safety.

Design guidelines for streetscape treatments can help to create a visible organizational structure and a sense of human scale. To ensure a sense of safety, visibility of the street from adjacent buildings should be maximized; public spaces should be designed to provide for unobstructed views; and adequate lighting of streets, public spaces, and parking areas should be provided. Activities on the street and in public spaces should be encouraged in order to create feelings of safety and security. A high level of main-

The high quality of the Portland streetscape is captured in this view of the various elements that contribute to the creation of a people-friendly environment. The walkway paving, flowers, street trees, and attractive storefronts complement one another to form a unifying pedestrian network in the city's retail district.

tenance to keep the city center clean and well organized also increases both physical and psychological comfort.

Principle 7: Emphasize High Quality

Simplicity of design, high-quality materials, and a high level of maintenance provide a tangible expression of concern for the quality of the pedestrian experience and extend an invitation for use of public spaces.

The highest-quality streetscape materials and street furniture affordable should be used, and top priority should be given to the fundamental elements of a high-quality public environment—paving, trees, lighting, and seating. The selection of materials and design treatments should reflect the need to minimize long-term maintenance costs, and these costs should be considered during the initial capital funding strategy. Guidelines and design review can promote high quality in public and private sector improvements.

Redesign of the pedestrian space on the Champs-Elysées in Paris—which included removal of service roadways that ran parallel to the street to expand the width of the walkways—provided additional paved area for outdoor cafés, street vendors, and pedestrians.

Central Park—a place where urbanites could taste all the joys of rural life, including seclusion, without leaving the city.

—Frederick Law Olmsted

CHAPTER 6

Public Spaces

The city center's public spaces provide opportunities for human interaction and enjoyment. When these public gathering places display a distinctive personality and add to the vitality of the central area street life, they are powerful catalysts for private investment.

The city center's most important public spaces are its streets—the space from building front to building front, including street pavement. Because of their visibility, streets can play a powerful role in building a positive, unified city image. Other types of public spaces, including parks, plazas, arcades, atriums, and galleries, also help to establish the city center's character as a place.

Creating a Successful Public Space

To be successful, a public space should do the following:

❖ *Soften and humanize the hard surfaces of the urban environment.* Ensuring that land in the intensively developed core is allocated to green space is a tangible way to express concern for human values. These spaces add pleasure and enjoyment to the city center experience, create visual interest, and provide attractive settings for leisure activity.

Central Park, New York City.

The plaza at Embarcadero Center in San Francisco, a popular meeting place in the heart of the office and financial district, features restaurants in the bases of the office buildings that open onto the large activity area and fountain. The tree canopy softens and humanizes the public space and provides shade for people enjoying an outdoor café.

❖ *Create settings for casual social interaction, civic gatherings, informal recreation, and special events.* The central area public spaces should make apparent the vitality and life of the city and invite participation and enjoyment. Through events programming, public spaces also can help to provide an expanded range of activities and attractions to draw people to the city center.

❖ *Establish elements that articulate the city center's physical structure.* City center public open spaces can be focal points in the urban structure if a consistent development pattern and a strong sense of place exist. However, these outdoor spaces cannot fulfill this role effectively until surface parking has been dealt with successfully. Surface parking creates gaps in the urban fabric and produces a random pattern of voids that dilute the impact of open spaces as a counterpoint to development.

❖ *Establish identity-building elements or place makers.* Public spaces can create a memorable image for the city center and serve as symbols of a healthy community social life, with different types of spaces helping to build identities for the central city's core and for related development subdistricts. These places also serve as amenities toward which adjacent development can be oriented.

The city center should have a variety of public spaces to meet a variety of visual and functional needs. These spaces should be linked to each other and to the central area pedestrian network to create an integrated system.

68

Elements of a Successful Central Public Place

When a beautiful place for people is created in the center of the city, that space is invested with special meaning; it becomes the city's heart, the place to be. There is great symbolic significance in creating a civic space at a central location: devotion of a portion of the city's most valuable land to public use and enjoyment shows that a clear emphasis has been put on the quality of life of residents and visitors. Such a central place also has a functional significance as a setting for leisure activity and the celebration of urban life in the heart of the city. A central space that is well designed and maintained also will enhance the economic value of the land around it. The elements essential to creating a successful place are good location, optimal size, programming that creates a people-friendly atmosphere, and design that promotes maximum use.

Location

The central public space should be located at a crossroads where the major pedestrian paths intersect. It should spatially relate to—or be near—the center of retail concentration in order to capitalize on that center's potential to attract and generate pedestrian activity. Also, the surrounding area should provide a mix of uses to ensure that activity will continue beyond the workday into evening hours and weekends.

Lafayette Park offers people a tranquil place in the center of Washington, D.C., with large lawn areas and fountains defined by pedestrian walkways, shade trees, and restored historic structures. People can sit in the sun (above) or enjoy the shaded walkways that encircle the green space (below).

Spring flowers inscribed in the green space create an interesting pattern in this formal park in Salzburg, Austria. The central fountain, the sculpture, and the gardens create a beautiful foreground for Mirabell Palace.

Size

The city center's central public space should be large enough to accommodate major entertainment and civic events, but not so large as to appear devoid of activity during nonpeak periods; it is easier to create a lively atmosphere and sense of vitality in smaller spaces. In cities where the density of development and the intensity of pedestrian use are limited, the central space should be conservatively sized. For special events in such spaces, adjacent streets can be closed to vehicular traffic to accommodate heavy attendance.

The heights of surrounding buildings and the degree of spatial enclosure they provide are key references for determining the optimal size of a central public space. Generally, the width of the public space, including abutting streets, should not be more than three times the height of surrounding buildings, if the public space is to be defined and enclosed. A central focal point such as a sculpture or water feature can serve as an organizing element and provide a sense of scale that helps to define the space. A water feature also can create a sense of movement and activity, even when few people may be present.

Programming

A lively, people-friendly atmosphere is possible when the edges of the central public space are lined by retail shops, restaurants, and cafés. Experience has shown that one of the best ways to maximize use of public space to include com-

Redesign and development of Bryant Park in New York City included construction of a new restaurant and an outdoor café. Introduction of this commercial space on the eastern edge of the park activated the area, drawing hundreds of people during the day and into the evening, making it a safer place for other park users wishing to enjoy the public space.

Copley Square in Boston is an example of excellent park design and development. The central green was redesigned as a flexible activity space to accommodate outdoor concerts, festivals, and other public functions. A double row of shade trees encloses the space on two sides and helps frame the view of Trinity Church.

mercial activities, especially food service. Food draws people, and people enjoying themselves act as magnets for more people. Retail activity not only helps to energize the public space, but also creates a sense of surveillance and security. Presentation of concerts, art exhibits, festivals, and other such events is essential to capitalize on the potential of a central place to draw people to the city center. The most successful public spaces are usually maintained and programmed by a business improvement district (BID) or a nonprofit organization.

Design

The design of the central place must enhance its capacity to attract and accommodate a variety of activities. The primary design considerations include the relationship between the public space and the adjacent streets and walkways, the type and amount of seating provided, the potential for flexible use, the level of physical and psychological comfort, the number of amenities, and the amount of attention paid to providing high quality.

Relationship to the Street. The public space must have maximum visibility and accessibility from the street. People enjoy watching pedestrians walk along the street, and the presence of people visible within the space draws other people. Visibility is also important for security.

To attract potential users to the space, the transition between the street and the public space must be as simple as possible. For example, a consistent ground elevation should be maintained, or broad, shallow steps can be used when vertical changes are necessary. The sense of separation between the open space and the street elevation must be minimized.

Brick walkways that define Copley Square's central green provide space for vendors to market their fresh produce and craft items. The walkways extend to the street, allowing visual and physical access from paths around the park.

71

The café tables and chairs in this Tampa, Florida, plaza allow people to relax and enjoy the courtyard provided by the private property owner. The water features, shade trees, and outdoor furniture have made this a special place for people to gather.

Comfortable folding canvas chairs available in London parks are popular because people can arrange them to converse with friends, enhancing social interaction in the public space.

Comfortable Seating. One of the most important factors influencing the use of public space is the number and variety of opportunities for seating. Adequate seating area should be provided; typically, one linear foot (0.3 meter) of seating space for every 30 square feet (2.8 square meters) of plaza area is recommended. Seating can be built into the space in the form of steps, walls, and ledges. But the use of fixed individual seating should be avoided; movable chairs, in addition to conventional benches, allow users maximum flexibility in choosing where to sit in relation to the space, other people, and the sun.

Flexible Use. Designers and managers of the central place should avoid dictating single, specific uses for it, such as use as an amphitheater with fixed seating that is occupied only during special events. Nor should the central place be cluttered with a large number of fixed elements: to maximize flexibility, use of raised planters and other large fixed furniture elements should be avoided, especially in the center of the space. Broad paved areas should be provided where intensive pedestrian activity is anticipated, and the use of flush tree grates is recommended to protect roots from compaction, to create a unified space, and to provide visibility for a sense of security.

Comfort. The public space should include trees that are large enough to create a sense of scale and a canopy providing shade. The area under the canopy tends to become the zone most intensively used for informal activities such as meeting friends and people-watching. In warmer climates, darker paving materials can be used to reduce glare and heat reflection. To extend use of the space in spring and fall and to ensure summer comfort, sunny and shaded areas should be provided. It is especially important to provide access to the sun during periods of peak use—weekdays from noon to 2 p.m. when people like to sit on chairs or blankets placed on public lawns—by considering and, if possible, controlling the shadow patterns created by adjacent high-rise buildings. The potential for tall buildings to create wind-tunnel effects and downdrafts also should be considered.

Psychological comfort within the public space will be enhanced if programming generates activity and the space is designed

The programming of the public space at Boston's historic Quincy Market generates activity and business for merchants and street vendors operating there, attracting large crowds during the summer to shop, eat, and be entertained. Restaurants in the market buildings open onto the plaza, adding to the place's vitality.

to make that activity visible from the street. Plantings of intermediate height of three feet (one meter) or taller, screen walls, buildings, fixed furniture, and changes in elevation should be introduced with the utmost care because of their potential to limit visibility and create insecure areas within the public space.

Amenities and Delight. Use of special paving materials will create a sense of richness, texture, and visual interest. Fountains and reflecting pools, banners, and public art including sculpture should be included to stimulate and please the senses, enhance the environment, create meaning, and recall community history.

High Quality and Simplicity. It is important in the design of the public space to recognize that high quality at all scales, from the overall concept to the smallest detail, increases user enjoyment and appreciation. Use of the highest-quality materials possible and the highest quality of detailing will provide an expression of concern for human values, as well as for durability and maintainability, and will serve as a symbol of a com-

munity that has confidence in its long-term prosperity.

The most successful public spaces that serve as people places are designed simply: they do not command the user's attention, dictate use patterns, or rely on design gimmicks. Instead, they provide a supportive setting for activity.

Lafayette Park in Washington is an example of excellent urban design, with its green space and walk system laid out to contribute to the experience people have when visiting. The simplicity of overall design, selection of specimen trees, and use of high-quality paving materials make it relatively easy to maintain the park at a high standard.

A number of small urban parks have been created to enhance the residential/mixed-use neighborhood between Chicago's North Michigan Avenue and Lake Shore Drive. These linear spaces connect to a series of plazas and to the Chicago River, providing residents and visitors with an attractive link to hotels, stores, restaurants, and Chicago's waterfront amenities.

Other Public Spaces

Other public spaces can complement and support the core's central place and build a special identity for the subdistricts. These secondary public spaces can act as links among districts, entrance markers, amenities, and catalysts for private development.

Design and Location

The design of these other public spaces should employ all the elements required to create a successful central place and at a scale appropriate to the size of the space. Activity and vitality can be fostered through the incorporation of food vendors and programmed edges and by maximizing accessibility and visibility from the street. In addition, an ample quantity of and choice in seating must be provided. These qualities will ensure that the spaces are appealing and well used.

The location of these public spaces is also important. They should relate to pedestrian walkways and larger public areas as part of an integrated system. In addition, they should capitalize on the higher levels of activity that occur where pedestrian paths intersect.

Plazas

Plazas developed in association with office buildings frequently are not integrated into the city center's patterns of pedestrian movement. These spaces can create adverse impacts by interrupting the active shopping frontage along streets or by separating uses that should reinforce one another. Many plazas destroy the streetwall formed by the architecture

The urban plaza in front of Seattle's Westlake Center provides space for outdoor activities and special events. The new public space, created by closing a street for one block, is important because it helped to define the center of the retail district and established a sense of place in the heart of the city center.

74

along the right-of-way and undermine the sense of structure and visual continuity. It is also possible to have too many plazas and not enough activity to fill them.

If a density bonus program exists to encourage private developers to create public amenities, the public sector should maintain control over the location and design of public plazas. Should the public sector plan to require a public plaza at a development, it first should be readily apparent how the plaza will provide the elements outlined above for successful public spaces. If a plaza is proposed at a specific location where these elements cannot be employed, the public sector should encourage the developer to contribute to open-space development at a different location where the benefits of public space would be more certain.

Parks

Parks and linear open spaces contribute to city center livability by creating refreshing counterpoints to the urban setting. These green spaces, which provide opportunities for informal recreation and are important image builders, can be especially influential in creating a positive environment for city center residential development. Design emphasis should be placed on establishing a high-quality lawn with tree plantings—and a water feature, if there is enough space. Use of limited shrub plantings will simplify maintenance and avoid creation of hidden spaces that can cause security problems. Only a few accents such as a colorful floral panel, a sculpture, or a fountain are needed; simplicity in design is the key to success.

The importance and potential visual impact of open spaces located at the edge of rights-of-way, especially at the entrances to the central area, should not be forgotten. High-quality landscape design and maintenance at these locations create a positive image and make the gateway a welcoming place.

Improvements to Central Park over the past ten years have made it more attractive to the people of New York City. One of the most successful spaces is the Sheep Meadow, an area reserved for passive recreation, picnicking, and sunbathing.

Broad boulevard medians and park squares that are part of the street pattern yield opportunities to create visual amenities, a positive neighborhood identity, and a recreational resource for in-town residential areas. These green spaces also can work as pedestrian connections that link neighborhoods to the central core.

The parks and landscaped parkway along the Charles River are part of an impressive greenway system that runs through Boston and Cambridge, Massachusetts.

75

Waterfronts

Cities with a central area waterfront possess a special open-space opportunity because water edges are natural magnets for people and can become valuable recreational and visual resources. A waterfront also can provide a prestigious address for private development. Land use policies and development standards should ensure that the economic development potential of waterfront areas is fully realized and that opportunities for public use and enjoyment and environmental protection are provided.

The scale and character of waterfront development must be carefully managed to avoid creation of a wall that blocks access and views; pedestrian amenities and high quality at the ground level are a must. Private sector cooperation is essential in creation of waterfront promenades lined with activities and public access easements to the waterfront. The linear edge of the waterfront development should be punctuated by public spaces and open views.

Attractive and clearly defined pedestrian connections between the waterfront and the city center's retail spine are critically important if the appeal of the waterfront is to extend into the core; visual and physical access to the water should be preserved along streets that terminate at the water's edge. Also, vehicular access to the site, particularly during nonpeak seasons, is important to the success of the waterfront.

The Royal Botanic Gardens in Sydney, Australia, overlook the harbor, the Sydney Opera House, and the Harbour Bridge. This city center park, which contains a wide array of exotic and native trees and flowers that thrive in a temperate climate, is linked to the opera house and the city center by a waterfront promenade.

Interior Public Spaces

Galleries, atriums, and arcades provide interior social spaces and pedestrian connections that make the city center more interesting and enjoyable for office workers, shoppers, residents, and visitors. Light, plants, water features, storefronts, and cafés can energize these spaces to create a marketable identity for individual projects and to add a new dimension to the city center. Visibility and accessibility from the street are crucial to ensuring that interior public spaces are well used; ideally, they can link directly to outdoor spaces and streets and create a feeling that all public spaces are part of a single environment.

Public/Private Hybrids

A new breed of interior public space that combines elements of the traditional shopping arcade with the modern office entrance lobby has evolved into a key aspect of successful office and mixed-use development. These new spaces, which blend public and private elements, usually take the form of an atrium that provides seating, water and landscape features, and retail activity. While using these spaces to make a development more competitive in attracting tenants or buyers, the private sector is also meeting the need for public gathering places that have many amenities, are protected from the elements, and can be used year-round.

To add to the city center character as a place for people, these spaces should look and feel "public" and must be designed as an integral part of the public realm. They also should be viewed as a complement to, not a replacement for, outdoor public

spaces. Still, no matter how carefully these spaces and their entrances are designed, they tend to create a screening effect that discourages use by some segments of the population. Retail centers that were designed with interior spaces and lack adequate connection to the external public realm have lost market appeal.

The historic Euclid Avenue Arcade in Cleveland, Ohio, (top) was one of the first retail arcades built in North America. The Eaton Centre retail galleria in Toronto, Canada, (above) is an excellent example of a public space that was designed and constructed with private funds.

77

In the most successful retail centers, the interior space is designed to link visually with the external environment. Use of glass in entrances and in the space above the stores gives people the feeling of being outdoors. This retail center in the Back Bay of Boston has also benefited from the restoration of the Copley Square public realm.

Avoiding Unwanted Effects

Interior public spaces should be designed so as to avoid siphoning pedestrian activity from the street and capturing it in the interior of buildings. In the core area, interior public spaces work best if they have multiple entrances connecting to existing streets and buildings so they can provide a shortcut between blocks and a place where people can linger and socialize. While links between interior spaces and parking structures are often viewed as amenities, care should be taken to limit such links because people then may avoid city streets and the pedestrian environment. The design of these structures should limit the ability of visitors to come

to the city center by car, enter a single enclosed garage or building, and never emerge onto the street.

Design Principles

The principles for designing successful interior public spaces address the same issues involved in designing other public places. They include:

❖ Make the space highly visible from the street through the use of multistory, transparent facades and easily visible entrances.

❖ Provide ample seating with a range of choices in how people relate to one another and to the space's ambient activity—i.e., both fixed and movable seating located in or away from the stream of activity.

❖ Provide liberal landscape plantings to create a sense of human scale and an amenity.

❖ Employ as much natural lighting as possible, using skylights, transparent facades, and clerestory windows to provide even illumination levels throughout the space.

❖ Design for vertical emphasis by creating a space that is higher than it is broad, ideally with two or three floors of adjoining buildings opening into the interior space.

❖ Provide public uses and activities such as food sales, newsstands, and retail shops on the edges of the space.

❖ Create links to exterior public spaces and the pedestrian system.

Sony Center at Berlin's Potsdamer Platz provides office, retail/restaurant, and entertainment space; condominium units; rental apartments; and parking. Located in the heart of the city, the Potsdamer Platz project has altered Berlin's landscape dramatically, leading the way in restoring the area's preeminence as a cultural and retail center.

The Downtown Denver Partnership is responsible for management and maintenance of the 16th Street transitway, street amenities, and other public spaces in the city center. High-quality maintenance has changed the popular perception of central Denver and numerous other city centers in the United States and Canada.

Public Space Management and Maintenance

Centralized management, including special events programming, will increase the ability of public spaces to attract people and make the city center a lively, dynamic, and interesting place. BIDs can provide such management to ensure that a consistently high level of maintenance is provided, leading to clean, well-tended public spaces that invite appropriate use and convey an image of high quality. Patterns of public space use need to be reevaluated periodically to gauge the effectiveness of the original design and to provide for timely changes and additions that will enhance use and enjoyment. Maintenance programs also should be reviewed and modified as needed, but investment in good design and high-quality, durable materials is the best strategy for minimizing maintenance problems.

The business improvement district staff in Washington, D.C., (left) provides assistance to visitors seeking information on tourist attractions, commercial services, and public transportation. In Columbia, South Carolina, (bottom) the City Center Partnership formed hospitality teams to create a cleaner, safer, and better-managed central area.

Streets and their sidewalks, and the main public places of a city, are its most vital organs.

—Jane Jacobs

CHAPTER 7

Pedestrian Realm

To attract a diverse and concentrated mix of uses and foster economic interaction among these uses, the city center must encourage pedestrian movement through the central core. Consequently, a key element of revitalization planning is to establish an attractive system of pedestrian connections.

Planning of the city center pedestrian system begins with recognition of and improvements to the core area's central spine—the street where the greatest concentration of retail activity already exists and where new retail uses should be located. But a successful central area should have more than one pedestrian-oriented shopping street: needed is a system of pedestrian connectors linking major activity anchors to the spine and to one another.

System Components

The primary elements of the city center's pedestrian network should be on the street, sharing the rights-of-way with vehicular traffic. Developing on-street linkages is the most practical and cost-effective approach to creating this pedestrian network because it works within the framework already established by existing development patterns, maintains business visibility, and eliminates the need for street closures.

Morrison Street, Portland, Oregon.

also might be designed as a transitway or a pedestrian mall. In all cases, however, this spine should be readily identifiable as the city center's primary corridor by its concentration of retail activity and its streetscape treatment. It should constitute the central area's 100 percent retail location, stand out as the most richly designed component of the pedestrian system, portray the city's central image, and be the focus of activity.

Ideally, major anchors should be located at each end of the spine to maximize the volume of pedestrian use along its length and to create an attractive retail setting. In larger cities, such a spine might encompass a sequence of "anchor-to-anchor" settings. The central spine should include a balanced mix of retail, office, hotel, entertainment, and residential uses to ensure a cycle of activity that extends to

Establishment of a high-quality pedestrian environment along the central spine of the city center contributes to its physical and economic regeneration. In Chicago, development of the streetscape and seasonal plantings on North Michigan Avenue has established a high-quality image for the retail and commercial businesses on the street.

Because most of the city center's pedestrian system consists of on-street components using shared rights-of-way, the system must be planned in coordination with the classification of streets as the spine, primary connectors, secondary connectors, and through-block connectors.

The Spine

In most cities, the central spine will accommodate both pedestrian and vehicular traffic; in certain circumstances, it

Outdoor cafés enrich and enliven pedestrian walkways in the city center. This street in Toronto, Canada, shows the ambience created when restaurants are permitted to use a portion of the walkway for outdoor dining. Most cities receive rental income for use of this valuable public space, providing funds that can be used to maintain and enhance the pedestrian realm.

evenings and weekends. In addition, the spine is the priority location for street vendors, cafés, outdoor performances and displays, and for special design components, including paving and streetscape elements, public art, and water features.

Primary Connectors

The primary connectors are the streets that serve as major pathways for pedestrians. As the name implies, they provide the primary physical connections among the city center's activities and amenities and, through their streetscape treatment, create a clear visual structure for the central area. Like the spine, they should be designed to encourage pedestrian activity. Primary connectors, in turn, can be the amenity spines of subdistricts outside the core, providing a catalyst for private investment and new development.

Secondary Connectors

Secondary streets, the remaining streets within the city center core, usually are used as service arteries, transit corridors, and access roads leading to major parking areas. Although they are less important for pedestrian circulation than the spine or the primary connectors, their streetscape treatment should provide at least a minimum level of comfort for people on foot.

Through-Block Connectors

Through-block connectors are pedestrian pathways located at street level but off the street that provide shortcuts through development blocks. They function most effectively when they complement and reinforce the spine and primary connectors by running perpendicular to and providing links between them. Where the

The central spine can be as vital in a small town as in the central area of a large city, with creation of a high-quality pedestrian environment stimulating private investment in the retail shops and storefronts in the community's town center.

development pattern creates long blocks, through-block connectors can become especially important features of the pedestrian system by adding to the convenience of movement within the core. They can also function as linkages between parking and the major retail streets. Such through-block connectors add texture, richness, and diversity to the city center experience, and also can expand the potential for retail activity within the core by creating new retail frontage.

The historic arcade in Norfolk, Virginia, which provides a through-block link between two important streets in the city center, is used by many people to reach their destinations in the office district or on the waterfront. Most through-block connectors were designed as retail arcades, but the lack of adequate pedestrian traffic can make it difficult to sustain retail uses.

This pedestrian-oriented street in Dusseldorf, Germany, illustrates how simplicity and consistency in streetscape design contributes to a high-quality shopping experience (above). The streetscape elements, trees, benches, and flowers are usually located in the curbside planting zone so that the amenities do not distract from the visibility and appeal of the storefronts (below).

Design Considerations

The primary considerations in designing the components of the city center pedestrian system are use of the streetscape to create an attractive and comfortable setting for pedestrian activity, appropriate allocation of space to pedestrians and vehicles in shared rights-of-way, and creation of a positive relationship between the street and the development that defines its edge.

Streetscape
Streetscape treatment on the spine and primary connectors should create a unified image and defined visual structure

for the city center, as well as an inviting and comfortable pedestrian environment. Simplicity and consistency are the keys to design success: simple design concepts executed with the highest-quality materials hold up best over time in terms of both maintenance and visual appeal.

The design of the streetscape should emphasize the linear continuity of the street space and enhance its potential for flexible use. The streetscape should establish an attractive foreground for businesses and a setting for other city center activity by creating an environment that is visually satisfying but that does not detract from the visibility and appeal of storefronts.

Walkway Width
A walkway pavement width of 20 feet (six meters) is desirable along the pedestrian spine and primary connectors. That width provides for both a 12-foot (3.7-meter) pedestrian zone adjacent to storefronts—to accommodate both window-shopping and through movement—and an eight-foot (2.4-meter) amenity zone adjacent to the curb. A walkway 20 feet (six meters) wide will allow seating, outdoor cafés, and public art to be incorporated into the streetscape without encroaching on the pedestrian zone. Streets used for mass transit require an amenity zone that is an additional ten to 15 feet (three to 4.6 meters) wide to accommodate queuing areas and shelters at the curb. Where the potential volume of pedestrian use is lower—i.e., secondary connectors or streets in smaller cities—walks that are more than 14 to 16 feet (4.3 to 4.9 meters) wide can dilute the sense of vitality and activity in the core.

Walkway Paving

The use of special paving on the spine and primary streets has a tremendous impact on the sense of amenity and visual richness. When used consistently, special paving also provides a visual connecting element that reinforces the pedestrian system. Although its initial installation cost is higher than for poured-in-place concrete, the durability and impact of special paving make it worth the expense. It is important not to lose sight of the first rule for all paving: it should be walkable in all weather for people of all ages in all types of footwear; uneven paving, shallow curbs, and steps can create safety hazards and discourage pedestrian activity.

A single special paving material should be selected for use throughout the pedestrian network. It can be used on the full width of the walk along the spine from storefront to curb, or in the curbside amenity zone as an accent to complement concrete walks on primary connectors. On all secondary connectors, plain concrete paving is recommended. Special paving also can be used to define pedestrian crosswalks to make them highly visible to motorists. In colder climates, special attention should be paid to whether snow removal equipment might damage modular paving in the crosswalks. The most successful pedestrian crossings are those used throughout Europe created with bold stripe patterns applied to the street paving to attract the attention of motorists.

Many cities have discovered the benefit of using concrete and clay pavers on city center walkways. In Washington, (above) developers are required to use two-by-three-foot (0.6-by-0.9-meter) paving blocks when replacing existing poured-in-place concrete. The scoring pattern and color used in the pavement on State Street in Chicago (left) is an environmental amenity that encourages pedestrian activity on this retail corridor.

85

Wide setbacks along Pennsylvania Avenue in Washington provide space for a double row of street trees and sites for street vending and outdoor cafés (above). Parisian-style benches and colorful paving add to the richness of this ceremonial street (below).

Plantings

Canopy street tree plantings are one of the city center's most important streetscape features. They create a consistent, high-quality foreground for the motorist's perspective and establish a sense of separation between the street's traffic lanes and the pedestrian zone. In addition, street trees provide shade, create a human scale that tempers the large buildings, and enhance pedestrian comfort without obscuring the visibility of storefronts.

Although raised planters have been used extensively to increase the sense of separation between the walkway and the adjacent street, they limit the amount of space for pedestrians and the potential for multiple uses for the curbside amenity zone. In addition, they can give pedestrians the sense that the street is cluttered and add to streetscape construction and maintenance costs. For these reasons, their use is not recommended unless they provide the only way to create planting areas over subsurface vaults or utility lines. If colorful floral accents are desired as part of the streetscape, movable planters can be provided at intervals within the curbside zone, but it is essential that an adequate annual budget be provided for seasonal planting and maintenance.

Street Furniture

The use of well-designed furniture throughout the central area helps to establish a unifying theme. Regeneration planning must incorporate criteria for the selection and use of streetlights, seating, trash receptacles, newspaper vending machines, movable planters, transit shelters, tree grates, and vendor carts. These criteria also should guide the design and location of regulatory and directional signs to minimize their visual impact and enhance legibility. Also needed are criteria that set standards for the use and location of public art, such as sculptures, murals, and banners.

Pedestrian-scale lighting, employing 12-foot-high (3.7-meter-high) light standards, should be used wherever possible to establish a high-quality amenity along pedestrian streets. These lower, human-scale lights can be used between intersections lit by standard-height street-

lights to provide a uniform illumination level that increases security without creating harsh light or glare.

While ample, well-designed seating is important in order to increase the level of pedestrian comfort, the curbside is not always the best location for it. Except for bus stops and outdoor cafés, areas adjacent to the walkway but set back from the street are more appealing sites for seating than the curbside amenity zone. As part of the design of buildings, plazas, and parks, seating opportunities can be provided using ledges, steps, low walls, movable tables and chairs, and conventional benches.

Streetside seating can best be accommodated where the pedestrian amenity zone allows sufficient space for benches arranged perpendicular to the roadway. This arrangement provides opportunities for people-watching; benches facing away from the pedestrian zone and toward the street are only useful for transit patrons. Simply

designed wood or steel benches that combine comfort and durability should be selected. If the funding is not available to purchase the highest-quality benches, it is probably best not to use them on the street at all.

Dedicated Pedestrian Streets

In the 1960s, many architects and planners believed that complete separation of pedestrian and vehicular movement would create the most attractive environment for people and best serve the city center retailers. Cities in the United Kingdom, continental Europe, and Australia developed dedicated pedestrian streets to serve their expanding city center retail markets. In North America, the pedestrian mall was introduced to help save declining retail districts that were being outperformed by the suburban malls, which offered pedestrian amenities and free parking.

The narrow pedestrian streets in York, England, (left) are inviting due to the scale of the space, the presence of retail shops, and the high quality of the historic buildings. In Bayreuth, Germany, (right) the wide rights-of-way provide space for produce markets, street vendors, and outdoor cafés. The activities and programmed events that take place in these dedicated pedestrian streets are critical to their success.

The Third Street Promenade in Santa Monica, California, was designed to emphasize the qualities of a traditional street, a sense of human scale, and the linear continuity of the public right-of-way. Thousands of people from the Los Angeles area are attracted to this high-quality pedestrian street that provides residents and visitors with an interesting mix of retail and entertainment choices.

❖ a merchandising mix that is more competitive with suburban centers;

❖ links among all the city center's major generators to foster market synergy among uses; and

❖ street access and visibility, which are eliminated when a mall is created.

Although the pedestrian mall concept attracted shoppers, it failed to keep them coming back because its land use and retail mix were weak. Many pedestrian streets also failed largely because their design—especially in the earlier years—ignored the special character of the urban street. Instead of emphasizing the traditional street's architecture, sense of human scale, spatial enclosure, and linear continuity, the design of the pedestrian street often took the elements that characterized the public spaces of the suburban shopping center—berms, informal planting areas, raised planters, fixed seating, fountains, and play sculptures—and used them to fill the street space.

But subsequent studies of how people use urban spaces show that the exclusion of vehicular traffic or the separation of vehicular and pedestrian systems is not necessary or even desirable. Indeed, removing all vehicular traffic from selected streets or giving the street over to vehicles and creating a separate system of skywalks for pedestrian movement can be counterproductive.

Closing the city center's retail spine to vehicles and converting it to a pedestrian street was an inadequate response to the broader economic problem of how to strengthen the center's retail uses. The effort often failed not because the idea of enhancing the central area's identity as a place for people was misguided, but because the basic concept ignored a number of fundamental requirements for city center retail regeneration. These requirements include:

❖ new activity generators to draw more people to the central area, establishing a new base of market support;

Often, the scale of the pedestrian space created by closing the street to vehicles presented a problem. Compared with a traditional shopping area, the pedestrian street, when vehicles were excluded, seemed to be out of scale with the volume of pedestrians, leaving it looking empty rather than lively and bustling with activity. Many pedestrian streets also failed on a more detailed design level because they used paving materials, street furniture, and planting approaches that impaired the space's flexibility for use for a variety of functions, created a sense of visual clutter, and ignored the goals of durability and maintainability.

The application of suburban design concepts to city center spaces was destined to fail because it did not recognize the essential characteristics that make the urban street an attractive and social space. Most U.S. cities removed their pedestrian malls when public officials and property owners realized the need for accessibility and visibility. This failure carries two important lessons for designers of the city center's pedestrian system:

❖ It is dangerous to import imitative solutions unless the basic conditions that contributed to their original success are clearly present in the city center.

❖ The special characteristics and resources of the city center can enhance its identity, its sense of place, and its competitiveness without such imports.

Skywalk Systems

In the 1970s, a popular strategy to reduce conflicts between vehicular and pedestrian circulation in congested city centers was the grade-separated skywalk system. This proposed solution did not involve limiting traffic on certain streets to give the pedestrian priority, but rather luring most of the pedestrians off the street onto elevated skyways connecting the upper levels of the buildings. Grade-separated systems—which can also come in the form of tunnels—do offer some benefits that may be difficult to achieve by other means, including provision of pedestrian safety, as well as creation of climate-controlled walkway connections, of particular value in northern cities during the winter. But the serious disadvantages of such systems usually far outweigh these

This pedestrian bridge in San Francisco was designed to look like and have the feel of a traditional street. The introduction of café tables and chairs and colorful planters on the walkway adds to the positive experience of crossing between two second-level pedestrian plazas. In favorable climates, pedestrian bridges do not have to be enclosed.

Most pedestrian bridges have been constructed to provide climate-controlled walkways between office and retail development and related parking. In Cedar Rapids, Iowa, (right) and Minneapolis, Minnesota, (below) the second-level walkways are part of a city center skyway system. These interconnected walkways are widely used in northern U.S. cities, but they have hurt street-level retail business.

virtues. Among the disadvantages are the following:

❖ Development of a grade-separated system almost always depends on the willingness of private property owners to provide public corridors between or within their buildings and to help fund their construction. This frequently means that key connections are not developed in a timely manner and that public access is limited to particular segments.

❖ Significant problems can arise involving access to the skyway system from street

level, the visibility of entrance points, and connections between buildings with different elevations. Without suitable access, use of the entire system will be limited. Also, escalators or elevators must be provided to assist in making vertical connections. A number of cities have eliminated their skywalks because of the high cost of operating and maintaining the mechanical systems associated with the escalators and elevators.

❖ It is extremely difficult to maintain the architectural integrity of older buildings when skywalks are added. Skywalk bridges also block traditional view corridors along the streets, diminish the perception of connections between subdistricts and anchors, and weaken the overall visual integrity of the city center's urban personality.

❖ Skyway systems can present security problems. Segments may not be visible from the street and they often lack active storefront uses, making them difficult to patrol and making it hard for pedestrians to gauge their own safety. If the level of security is perceived to be low, people will not use the system.

❖ The most powerful argument against development of grade-separated pedestrian systems: they sap vitality from the street-level environment. Skywalk and underground systems tend to siphon retail and pedestrian activity from the street, isolating and ignoring the features that have the greatest potential to give the city center a lively atmosphere and sense of vitality.

Unless the intensity of pedestrian use and the potential support of retail expansion are especially strong, it is difficult or impossible to merchandise fully both at the street level and the skyway or underground level. Grade-separated systems ultimately can undermine the goal of creating a better street-level environment. Cities that already have lower intensities of street activity are especially vulnerable. Even in larger cities, the volume of pedestrian use needed to support continuous activity both on the street and within the grade-separated systems is usually found only in a small part of the city center.

Instead of separating pedestrian and vehicular flows through the use of skywalks or tunnels, city center planning should establish an appropriate balance between pedestrians and vehicles in the corridors they share. This means giving priority to the pedestrian on the spine and the primary connectors while providing a minimum number of pedestrian amenities on all other streets within the city center.

View corridors along important image streets can be impaired by construction of a major pedestrian bridge over a street right-of-way. The bridge in Norfolk (top) and the elevated walkway in Cedar Rapids (above) cross over important image streets that motorists use to enter the city center.

And the first lesson we have to learn is that a city exists, not for the constant passage of motor cars, but for the care and culture of men.

—Lewis Mumford

Vehicular Circulation

To strengthen the city center's attractiveness as a market and to support existing and new uses, strategies should be put into place to allow efficient access to the center for vehicles and transit. However, these strategies must reinforce rather than compromise the pedestrian environment.

Too often, peak-hour traffic and transit needs overwhelm the city center's core, weakening the continuity of street-level pedestrian activity and the quality of the pedestrian experience. Special attention must be paid to coordinated management of vehicular access, transit, and parking systems in order to ensure that the development pattern in the core is compact, integrated, and oriented toward the pedestrian.

Trade-offs to balance vehicle, transit, and pedestrian needs are almost inevitable and may involve difficult choices, but these choices must be made so that planning initiatives can be coordinated. Close cooperation among local, regional, and national agencies is required to ensure that transportation-related proposals will respond to the market, urban design visions, and plans for the city center.

Lake Shore Drive, Chicago.

State Street in Chicago is both a central spine and a major collector street, with a streetscape and wide walkways that provide a high-quality environment for retail and commercial activity. The amount of pavement devoted to vehicular circulation on this important, six-lane image corridor is substantial, but does not diminish the pedestrian experience.

Vehicular Hierarchy

The best way to strike a balance between a high-quality pedestrian environment and convenient vehicular and transit access is to establish a hierarchy of streets playing different roles, including major arterials, collectors, transitways, and local access streets.

The division of space between pedestrians and vehicles will be somewhat different for each street class. For example, major arterials that carry the heaviest traffic volumes can accommodate parallel pedestrian movement and crossing points, but the primary concern will be the safety and efficiency of traffic flow. In contrast, collector streets serve a more important

The central retail spine in Wiesbaden, Germany, also serves as a major collector street in the city center. Planners and transportation engineers in Germany collaborate to design and build streets that provide for vehicular access and circulation, but the pedestrian environment is never compromised to achieve transportation objectives.

pedestrian function, so they must provide a better balance between vehicle and pedestrian needs. The central spine and the local access streets will be the most important elements of the city center's pedestrian network; their design should give priority to the scale and number of amenities appropriate for the central area's most important people places.

The city center's functional hierarchy of streets should be visually reinforced through a hierarchy of streetscape treatments. A coordinated streetscape improvement program offers an outstanding opportunity to establish a clear physical structure, a sense of visual continuity, and a distinctive identity for the core area.

In planning improvements to the vehicular circulation system, the fundamental objectives are to do the following:

❖ provide good access to the city center;

❖ guide through-traffic around the intensively developed core area and route local city center traffic to major parking resources;

❖ provide convenient access for local traffic within the core; and

❖ facilitate orientation.

Once these objectives have been achieved, other initiatives for improving the efficiency of city center vehicular circulation should be carefully evaluated for their impact on the integrity of the existing development fabric and on the quality of the pedestrian environment. The most common mistake is to trade away the very characteristics that make the core area an attractive people place in exchange for optimal automobile circulation.

Major Arterial Streets

Major arterials are key entrances to the city center and should provide efficient access to the core and its surrounding subdistricts. Their design is geared primarily to the motorist, with priority given to carrying capacity, efficiency, safety, and visual continuity. As major gateways to the city center, arterial streets play an important role in defining the initial image of the city. The frequency of their use and the volume of traffic they carry reinforce their powerful influence on the overall image of the city center for visitors and residents, so creation of a positive

entrance identity on the gateway arterials should be given high priority.

Gateways and Edges

As major arterials approach the edge of the central core, they often pass through low-density fringe areas occupied by a mix of light industrial businesses, service stations, automobile repair shops, parking lots, strip commercial businesses, vacant land, and remnants of older neighborhoods. Because their visual image and environmental character typically are deteriorated, these areas create a negative entrance image for the city center rather than a positive one.

These edge areas should play a more positive visual and functional role as a transi-

The most important arterial roadway in Adelaide, Australia, is King William Street, the central spine for the office and financial district. This image street is enhanced by the streetscape and display of international flags in the median. On most arterial streets, the curbside lane is reserved for buses, taxis, and service vehicles rather than for on-street parking.

One of the most impressive views of Chicago's skyline is from Columbus Drive and Grant Park. This southern gateway, lined with trees and flags that invite residents and visitors into the heart of the city, provides an uplifting view of Chicago.

Many cities are rebuilding blighted and unused areas on the edge of the historic commercial core—land that often is adjacent to arterial streets that provide access to the city center. A number of outstanding residential projects on important arterial streets have been developed in Portland, Oregon.

An ideal way to rebuild urban neighborhoods is to construct new commercial space along the street while also providing a reasonable setback for the residential dwellings that face the roadway. This example in Portland illustrates the city's commitment to integrating retail services into the emerging neighborhoods at the edge of the city center.

tion between the city center and its adjacent neighborhoods and as a gateway to the more intensively developed central core. For example, they can accommodate housing at higher densities than is typical in established single-family neighborhoods and also can support office and institutional uses. The arterial frontage itself provides excellent visibility and the access needed for higher-density development.

Clearly articulated land use objectives for transitional areas, as well as public investment that improves the image of major arterial streets, will encourage new development and the upgrading of existing properties. Streetscape improvements are especially effective in creating a distinctive environment that serves as a catalyst for early private reinvestment in such gateway areas. Development controls,

applied through site plan review, for properties along these gateway arterials can help to ensure that new construction enhances the visual character of the street. Development that follows suburban models, especially regarding franchise businesses, is not appropriate for such locations, but frequently colonizes them anyway. Suburban and franchise development models place most of the parking in front of buildings, install signs that are too large in inappropriate locations, make little effort to relate to pedestrians, and apply strip commercial–style landscape standards along the right-of-way.

To prevent inner-city arterials from becoming poor cousins of their suburban strip commercial counterparts, some cities have implemented zoning and site development regulations for these roadways. Among the guidelines are the following:

❖ The primary orientation of major facades and building entrances should be toward the arterial street frontage.

❖ Strict limitations should be placed on development of parking between the building front and the street.

❖ Building frontyard and side-yard setbacks should decrease as the core is approached to create a progressively more intensive urban development pattern.

❖ Streetfront setbacks should be deep enough to create a broad, landscaped walkway that humanizes the pedestrian environment.

Access to the City Center

A network of major arterial streets should provide convenient access to each of the city center's subdistricts without funneling large volumes of traffic across them. Ideally, these arterials should serve as the boundaries of development subdistricts, framing areas within which pedestrian activity is encouraged to promote an integration of uses.

Arterial Loops. In a number of cities, an arterial loop has been used successfully to provide access to the edge of the central area while giving priority to the pedestrian within the core itself. However, it is important to remember that the core defined by the arterial loop must be large enough to incorporate a variety of uses and a critical mass of intensive development while maintaining a walkable radius of ten to 15 minutes.

The added traffic carrying capacity needed to introduce a loop system often can be created by removing on-street parking. In some instances, even greater carrying capacity may be required, which inevitably will lead to consideration of creating wider streets. However, the impacts of street widening on land use and the development fabric of adjacent districts, especially residential areas, can be disastrous: wider loop roads can become barriers to development if the traffic on them travels too fast or if the roadway is too difficult for pedestrians to cross.

A problem frequently encountered in implementing the arterial loop concept is how to avoid creating a moat of high-

traffic-volume streets that isolates the core from adjacent subdistricts. One strategy is to create clearly defined pedestrian connections across them.

In determining how these connections can be made, it often is assumed that only grade-separated crossings can be effective. On the contrary, the lower-cost solution of slowing and stopping traffic with pedestrian-activated crossing signals and providing broad crosswalks defined by special striping or paving is safer and more effective in encouraging pedestrian movement between the core and adjacent areas.

Application of the same paving treatment to the pedestrian walkways and the arteri-

Smaller cities can establish their image through high-quality lighting and streetscape improvements along access roads. The major access road to Baden Baden, Germany, leads motorists into the heart of the city with consistent directional signage and streetscape amenities (top). In Alexandria, Virginia, vehicles gain access to the retail district through an attractive office district (bottom).

97

al crosswalks makes it possible to enhance both the visual and functional continuity of the city center's system of pedestrian connections. If development adjacent to these crossing points is designed to create well-defined subdistrict gateways, it will provide an added incentive for the pedestrian to cross the arterial street.

Elevated and Below-Grade Highways.

In many cities, vehicular access to the core area was provided by construction of elevated or below-grade highways on the edge of the city center. However, these grade-separated roadways created major visual and environmental barriers between the central area and the adjacent neighborhoods and subdistricts. Some

cities have removed their elevated roadways or covered the below-grade versions and have replaced them with on-grade boulevards to provide vehicular access, thereby creating an economic stimulus to private investment in the neighborhoods and subdistricts around the central core.

Many historic districts have been separated from the central area by construction of elevated roadways. When these structures are removed, opportunities are created that restore and rebuild the neighborhoods or lead to creation of mixed-use developments that provide new housing and employment in the heart of the city.

Most cities in the United Kingdom, continental Europe, and Australia have designed and constructed on-grade boulevards and multilane arterial streets to provide vehicular access to the city center. These roadways are designed to be pedestrian friendly and to create visual and physical connections that link the city center, residential neighborhoods, and subdistricts that enhance the central area. Most of the major highways are constructed outside the city center and inner-city neighborhoods to minimize the impact of the automobile on the urban environment.

Within the Central Core

In some cases, major arterials cut through the central core and serve as both an important pedestrian street and as a high-volume traffic carrier. To provide an adequate sense of separation between the street's pedestrian zone and its traffic lanes, a broad curbside amenity zone is needed. A double row of street trees planted in this zone will steer pedestrians closer to the development edge and away from the traffic.

A boulevard median planted with shade trees also can soften the expanse of pavement and create a special identity for the arterial as a ceremonial street or a roadway providing a prestigious address. But even if attention is paid to every detail of visual character and pedestrian appeal, a street of this type will not facilitate pedestrian movement between blockfaces.

While it can serve as an attractive location for office or residential development, it will never represent an optimal retail setting because the distance between the sides of the right-of-way limits pedestrian movement.

One-Way Streets

One-way streets in the central area—which inevitably allow faster-moving traffic—harm street-oriented retail and commercial enterprises. Increased speed, noise, and pollution on multilane, one-way streets diminish pedestrian safety and comfort, which reduce business for stores and restaurants that depend on pedestrians for business. In contrast, offices and service-oriented commercial activity can benefit from sites along major one-way streets if the speed of the traffic is not excessive. Regardless, due to the speed of vehicular traffic, safe access for

This wide pedestrian amenity zone in Seattle, Washington, provides a sense of separation of the on-street parking and the one-way traffic from the adjacent retail stores. The double row of street trees improves the pedestrian experience, and the additional walkway width benefits shop owners who often lose business when two-way streets are converted to higher-speed one-way arterials.

motorists entering and exiting off-street parking areas is often a problem.

More and more cities are converting their one-way streets back to two-way roadways to reduce the speed of traffic, improve vehicular circulation, and restore a better balance between meeting the needs of autos and pedestrians within the city center. Traffic-calming strategies have proven to be successful in cities that are committed to creating a quality pedestrian environment: persuading vehicles to move slower allows people on foot or on bicycles to feel safe to walk or ride in the central area of the city.

Secondary Access Streets

Collectors and local access streets should serve as seams that unify opposite block-faces. While their design treatment will be determined by their specific circulation role, they should accommodate and encourage pedestrian use, especially when they serve as walkway connections between important activity generators.

Collector Streets

As the name implies, collector streets collect and distribute traffic between arterials and local streets. Like arterials, they provide good access and visibility, making them attractive locations for offices, entertainment venues, and higher-density housing developments. However, collector streets should provide a better balance between meeting pedestrian and vehicular needs than do arterials.

Although the number of traffic lanes and the amount of on-street parking may vary on different collector streets, the pedestrian zone—the area between the curb and the inside edge of the walkway—ideally should be at least 15 feet wide. Depending on the land use orientation and development intensity of the subdistrict within which the collector is located, the pedestrian zone can be treated either as an urban streetscape with pavement extending from the building front to the curb, or as a linear green space with a planting strip between the curb and the walkway.

When the adjacent land use is residential, the streetfront setback should be expanded

The transit-oriented streets constructed in Portland and in other U.S. cities have succeeded in allowing buses to move through the city at higher speed for the convenience of riders. But limiting automobile access on important commercial streets in the city center has hurt sales for merchants, and building owners have had difficulty leasing valuable streetfront property.

to provide additional green space between the street and the building facade. Street trees planted at regular intervals and at a uniform distance from the curb should be part of the streetscape treatment.

Where the collector also serves as an important pedestrian connection between activity anchors, special paving accents, pedestrian-scale lighting, public art, and street furniture will heighten the collector street's identity as an important link in the city center pedestrian system.

Transit Streets

Streets used for mass transit, which can attract extremely large numbers of pedestrians, require special attention to the quality of design for the pedestrian environment. Where they carry significant numbers of commuters into the core, transit streets offer opportunities for high-density development that does not depend upon large areas for support parking. Such transit corridors can stimulate economic development in office and other employment districts and in areas where major sports and entertainment venues are located. While retail districts benefit from the introduction of shuttle

transit service on pedestrian-friendly streets, the operation of large buses or light-rail transit on such streets can have the opposite effect.

Local Access Streets

These streets can be residential, commercial, or service oriented, and their design treatment should vary accordingly. With relatively low volumes of slower local traffic, these streets offer the greatest potential for developing a high-quality pedestrian environment. Where these streets serve major retail concentrations or serve as important linkages between city center anchors, they should be given the highest-quality streetscape treatment possible.

Never doubt that a small group of thoughtful, committed citizens can change the world; indeed, it's the only thing that ever has.

—Margaret Mead

Public Transit

In many cities, public transit is essential if the city center is to accommodate expanded and intensified development without creating unacceptable commuter-related traffic and parking demands. A transit strategy that brings large numbers of people to the central area then moves them through the core on foot helps the city center to avoid traffic congestion and overcrowded commuter parking. Transit links within the central area also may be needed when distances between complementary anchors prevent the development of effective pedestrian connections.

Commuter-Oriented Transit

Peak volumes of commuter traffic represent the prime stress on capacity for the city center street system. Commuter traffic also requires the dedication of significant amounts of city center land for parking. In many cities, these traffic and parking demands have come to limit, rather than expand, central area growth potential. For any significant amount of new development to occur in these cities, the balance must shift away from the car to other modes of transportation.

Bahnhofstrasse, Zurich, Switzerland.

Denver, Colorado, was one of the first U.S. cities to purchase low-platform electric buses, used on the 16th Street transitway. This shuttle transit system, which operates on a five-minute headway and without charge to the bus patrons, transports thousands of people from bus terminals and light-rail stations to their destinations in the city center.

Even when short-term limitations on growth are not an issue, most central areas will benefit from increased transit use. The greater the rise in the number of people who arrive in the city center without their cars, the greater the increase in pedestrian activity will be, adding life and vitality to the street. In addition, the potential for creating a compact development pattern and a positive pedestrian environment is improved. In all but the smallest cities, the number of city center employees is sufficient to support a commuter bus system, as long as it is efficient, well marketed, and competitively priced. Certainly, most cities could benefit from a shift of commuters to van pooling or carpooling from driving in single-occupancy vehicles.

On Regent Street in London, buses operate in dedicated lanes next to the curb. Bicycles and taxis also can use this space, and cars are allowed to cross the lane to reach service areas, off-street parking, and secondary streets. The dedicated city center transit routes extend into surrounding communities to speed the flow of buses into the heart of the city.

Promoting Transit Use

If commuter transit is to be a viable option, more must be done to provide transit alternatives. To be effective, transit-planning initiatives must be undertaken in coordination with complementary policies for traffic, parking, and pedestrian circulation.

One way to reduce dependence on the automobile and induce transit use is to make automobile use less convenient and less efficient. Such a strategy often requires the adoption of firm controls on the location, supply, and cost of parking in the city center and cooperation from major employers in the form of subsidized or free transit passes and limits to on-site parking capacity.

In an effort to address traffic gridlock and pollution in central London, city officials levy a charge on entering vehicles. Income from the levy will be used to improve public transit in the city.

Shuttle Transit

Most cities will profit from transit planning initiatives that move people more efficiently within the central area. Shuttle transit that quickly and conveniently carries commuters from fringe parking locations to city center destinations enables long-term

parking to shift out of the core area. An attractive and convenient system of transit connections also can strengthen the interaction between the core's retail spine and other activity anchors.

More and more cities—among them Denver, Colorado, and Chattanooga, Tennessee—are introducing low-platform, electric shuttle buses to encourage people to travel between various districts within the city center. These smaller buses also complement and enhance the pedestrian realm in retail and entertainment districts. The experience of riding on historic trolleys—as found in San Francisco—can add to the excitement of the city center.

Transit Corridors

Transit corridors should be located where they channel the greatest number of people to and across—but not along—the principal retail and pedestrian spine. Major transit corridors routes must either intersect the spine or be located in a nearby parallel corridor. So that transit patrons can move directly into the city center's primary pedestrian network, the transit corridor should be located inside the major arterial street system that frames the core. Land use and transit planning also must be coordinated to ensure that the highest densities of development—usually office and multifamily housing, the major generators of pedestrian traffic —are located near transit corridors.

Creation of a major transit corridor on the city center's pedestrian spine may discourage retail activity and regeneration; this may seem counterintuitive, but

experience in several cities supports this conclusion.

Dedicated Transit Lanes and Streets

A lane or an entire street can be dedicated to transit use to increase the speed and reliability of service by giving transit vehicles priority. However, a constant flow of large buses in a dedicated curb lane or on a dedicated street can reduce rather than enhance the quality of the city center's environment.

While these problems can be eased through the use of buses equipped with better noise and emission controls, many cities are introducing alternative transit technologies— such as electric and natural gas buses, trams, and light-rail systems—that produce fewer negative impacts, in an effort to provide people with access to the heart of their city.

The light-rail lines in Portland, Oregon, operate in dedicated transit space adjacent to pedestrian walks, allowing comfortable, safe, and easy access to the transit vehicles. Cities that locate their transit lanes in the middle of the right-of-way place riders in a substandard environment and discourage ridership.

In European cities, light-rail transit lines are integrated into the public space to provide a high-quality environment for retail and office development. The outdoor cafés and markets adjacent to the light-rail line in Zurich provide an exciting public realm for people who live and work in the city.

To enhance bus ridership, the pavement needs to be expanded at transit stops to provide space for bus shelters and passenger queuing. In Portland, a transit amenity zone of ten to 15 feet (three to 4.6 meters) has been added to the width of the pedestrian walk, eliminating the negative impact often associated with bus stops located too close to storefronts.

Design of Transit Streets

The corridors that serve as commuter and shuttle transit routes inevitably will attract significant pedestrian use. These transit streets must include attractive pedestrian environments incorporating wide walkways, special paving, and street trees.

Transit corridors served by buses require special design treatments. One of the major considerations in locating a bus transit street is the width of the available right-of-way. In designing the busway, a minimum walkway and amenity zone of 25 to 30 feet (7.6 to 9.1 meters) should be provided to accommodate bus shelters and queuing areas. The added depth of the curbside amenity zone is also needed

to establish adequate separation between the bus lane and the pedestrian walkway.

Transit shelters should provide protection from the weather while allowing visibility of the shelter interior for security. Places to sit or lean should be provided as an integral part of the structure. As with other street furniture, transit shelters should have a simple design using high-quality materials if they are to remain attractive components of the center's visual environment over the long term.

Many cities have constructed bus transfer centers that link directly to the major city-wide transit corridors and are located within a five- to ten-minute walk of the core area. These transfer centers provide covered waiting space, passenger conveniences, and links to the larger transit network. Bus ingress, egress, and queuing can be planned so as not to interfere with auto and pedestrian movements on the surrounding streets.

Elevated Transit Systems

Where the city center's transit system must use city center streets to pick up, discharge, and move large numbers of people quickly during peak periods, conflicts with surface traffic movement can

In Charlotte, North Carolina, local and regional buses terminate their trips at this transfer facility, which allows people to walk to city center destinations or transfer to other forms of transportation. The protected waiting space, food service, and restrooms have made transit use more attractive.

cause unacceptable delays. As a result, transportation planners often look to elevated transit systems as a means of moving large numbers of riders with maximum speed and efficiency. However, elevated systems have significant impacts on the function and appearance of the central area, and on the cost of maintaining it. Among the impacts are the following:

❖ expenses involved with installing and maintaining stairs, escalators, and elevators to move transit patrons from street level to the station platform;

❖ problems with security and surveillance;

❖ creation of a separate, upper-level pedestrian system that siphons activity away from the street;

❖ high noise levels;

❖ darkened streets, blocked view corridors, and obscured building facades caused by elevated transit structures; and

❖ difficulties making areas under elevated transit structures appealing and attractive.

Because of these drawbacks, elevated systems are seldom an appropriate solution to the challenge of improving transit access to the city center. Every effort should be made to rethink and redesign the ground-level street system before such elevated systems are considered.

In Miami, Florida, the transit structure was built in the center of the city's most beautiful boulevard (top). In Seattle, the people mover was built down the center of an important commercial street, blocking the view corridor and shading much of the right-of-way (bottom).

Design is the human capacity to shape and make our environment in ways without precedent in nature, to serve our needs and give meaning to our lives.

—John Heskett

CHAPTER 10

Parking Facilities

Decisions about how to address the issue of parking are among the most important in making the city center a high-quality place for people. The city center cannot have a pedestrian orientation, a concentrated diversity of uses, or a continuity of street-level activity if parking is not well designed. Surface parking in particular can create large gaps in the development structure and isolate key uses from one another.

Although it is crucial to supply an adequate amount of convenient parking, it also is essential to minimize the land area required to do so. Especially in the center city where a retail core exists or can be created, preference should be given to short-term parking for retail patrons rather than to long-term parking for employees. To minimize the impact of parking on the visual quality of the streetfront, parking frontage on major arterials and key pedestrian streets should be curtailed. Wherever possible, parking should be located underground or in interior-block structures behind active uses.

Public parking, San Francisco.

Portland, Oregon, was one of the first U.S. cities to implement a public transportation policy designed to reduce dependence on the private automobile. The plan, which included construction of bus transitways on two north-south streets and light-rail transit running on two east-west streets, was linked to a policy that limited construction of new parking facilities in the city center.

Limiting Use of Long-Term Parking

Several cities have found they can support the expansion of office use while minimizing the need for long-term employee parking within the intensively developed core by implementing parking-related policies in concert with transit and transportation management initiatives. For example, in larger cities, the price of long-term parking within the core can be increased and the supply of commuter parking limited to encourage commuters to shift to use of transit. However, it is important to coordinate such major changes in parking policy with measures to upgrade the commuter transit system. Otherwise, the ability of the city center to attract and hold office and retail uses may suffer if people are forced to park too far from their desired destination.

Efforts to improve parking management also can be complemented by efforts to encourage carpooling, ridesharing, or "live-near-your-work" programs, or by subsidies for employee transit fares. Cities may even require participation in such transportation management programs—sometimes encouraged through city tax rebates or reductions—before new high-density office development is allowed. Higher densities should be located along or near transit corridors where they can be supported most efficiently by the transit system.

When a significant shift to commuter transit is not feasible, efforts to control growth in the city center's long-term parking demand can focus on management strategies that reduce the number of single-occupant vehicles by encouraging use of van pools and ride sharing. Moreover, a multiuse development approach that promotes residential uses along with office, retail, and entertainment can reduce parking demands by making it possible for a significant number of city center residents to walk or use local shuttle transit to reach work and shopping and leisure activities.

Allocating Resources Effectively

When allocating parking resources, close-in parking spaces should be dedicated to the most parking-sensitive functions. For instance, pricing and enforcement policies within the core area should give preference to retail patrons, business visitors, and other short-term users, although some flexibility should be maintained to accommodate close-in executive parking, which enhances the marketability of higher-end office space. Long-term employee parking must also be provided, though most of it should be located outside or on the edges of the core, but within a ten-minute walking distance. More distant fringe parking for commuters also can serve the core if attractive and efficient transit shuttles are provided.

When making decisions on parking resources, it is important to consider how modifications in the supply of long-term parking in the core area may affect adjacent neighborhoods. Where the central area parking supply is limited and priced to give priority to short-term parking, commuters and shoppers may search for free on-street parking in nearby neighborhoods, trading longer walks for money saved. To restrict the use of local residential parking areas, resident-only parking permit programs backed by strict enforcement may be needed to protect the quality of the residential environment. Land use policies also must stifle encroachment of surface parking into central area neighborhoods to support the core area's higher-density office development.

Expansion of surface parking into residential areas can quickly undermine neighborhood stability and diminish the mixed-use vitality that enables a strong city center to thrive as a regional hub.

Encouraging Construction of Parking Structures

The amount of surface area that must be devoted to parking in the core—and the impact it has on the city center and the areas around it—can be reduced through the construction of parking structures. Construction of parking structures can be encouraged through the provision of density bonuses by cities to developers who build such structures or through direct public assistance to finance or pay for their construction. However, there are limits to the economic feasibility of these approaches. Land values and development densities must be sufficiently high to support the costs of parking structures, which are much greater than costs for surface lots. Many smaller cities may only be able to afford one strategically located parking structure.

Many planners have proposed building large parking garages on the fringe of the city center, where land is not as valuable, and using small shuttle buses to transport people to the central area. In Chattanooga, Tennessee, the city constructed two large parking structures on the edge of the central core and purchased a fleet of electric buses to transport people to the retail, office, and institutional facilities in the city center.

In Alexandria, Virginia, the city owned a large surface parking lot behind the retail stores on King Street. Rather than build a freestanding garage on the valuable site, the city formed a partnership with a private developer to build a multistory residential building (at left in photo) which encloses three sides of a new parking garage.

Increasing Efficiency

While development financing and regulatory guidelines dictate specific parking requirements, a variety of measures can be put in place to increase parking efficiencies. Shared parking—parking used by businesses during the day and by others in the evening—is a more efficient use of space than parking dedicated exclusively to a single user. Appropriate off-street parking ratios for a variety of uses in the central area must be applied to make shared parking feasible, especially in the case of mixed-use developments. Parking requirements also can be reduced when transit service is provided and parking pricing is raised to make transit use more competitive economically.

Greater efficiency in the use of city center parking also can be promoted by giving the public sector or the business improvement district the responsibility for coordinating decisions on the development of shared parking areas. To be effective, a centralized parking management strategy must also establish limits on the amount of on-site parking to be provided by private developers. To make sure all private developers are paying their fair share to provide needed city center parking, they can make payments to the city in lieu of providing on-site parking. Public sector management of the city center's parking supply also can help to ensure that parking is provided in central locations where it can be shared by a variety of user types.

Construction of public parking can be funded in a number of ways, including general obligation or revenue bonds, special district assessments, tax increment financing, and developers' payments in lieu of on-site parking. Furthermore, the public sector can reduce the lease or sale price of publicly owned parcels as an incentive for a private developer to build and operate parking needed to foster and support a large-scale city center development.

Parking Location

The perception that there is a shortage of convenient parking in city centers often is based not on the actual supply of parking, but rather on a lack of awareness of its location and the absence of well-defined pedestrian connections between off-street or fringe parking facilities and city center destinations. Especially in smaller cities, shoppers tend to sense that the parking supply is inadequate and inconvenient unless they can find an on-street space either in front of the store or in a surface lot in the store's immediate vicinity. Because the suburban mall's parking is free and highly visible, users often ignore the fact that the walking distance between the car and the store entrance at the mall may be as great as, if not greater than, it is in the city center.

The facade of a parking facility should be designed to minimize the extent to which the structure interrupts retail continuity on important image streets. The open and transparent design of this parking structure in Karlsruhe, Germany, enhances the quality of the pedestrian realm on a secondary street.

The perceived inadequacies in the amount and location of city center parking can be largely overcome if the central area's identity as a multipurpose destination is made more readily apparent. A central core that is compact, with well-defined physical links between activities and a strong pedestrian orientation, will be seen as a one-stop activity center—a place where several activities can be accomplished on foot from a single parking space. Simple actions such as an easy-to-understand system of directional signs, location maps, and other "wayfinding" devices can eliminate much of the confusion that first-time visitors may confront when reaching the city center.

Of course, the parking available within convenient walking distance of the core's retail concentration should be dedicated to customers. Shoppers on retail-only trips need a sufficient supply of short-term parking near stores in on-street spaces, surface lots, and structures, and a uniform signage program to help them find such parking. Retail employees should not use these spaces for their own cars, as often happens. In addition, a validation program offering free parking to shoppers can enhance the perceived convenience of parking.

Pedestrian connections between parking and the core area's major anchors and retail spine should be attractive and convenient to use. Developers can help by providing through-block accessways that are edged by active uses. On the city center's principal retail spine, special efforts should be concentrated on upgrading rear facades and entrances to surface parking lots located behind retail establishments.

Parking facilities are often hard to locate because of inadequate directional signs. Mobile, Alabama, has designed an attractive signage system that advises motorists of the important buildings within walking distance of the parking structure. This sign is part of Mobile's comprehensive city center wayfinding system.

The design of street-level retail space and the parking structure's upper-floor facades can enhance the quality of the street and commercial uses served by the facility. The restaurant, retail storefronts, and the design of the entrance to this office building and parking structure all contribute to the environment on Los Olas Boulevard in Fort Lauderdale, Florida.

The size of parking facilities should be proportionate to the traffic carrying capacity of abutting streets. If possible, these facilities should not be located on the major arterial and primary pedestrian streets because of the important role these roadways play in shaping the city center's visual image and pedestrian circulation.

Parking Design Considerations

City center parking should be designed to improve the quality of the visual environment and to minimize the extent to which it disrupts movement among retail uses and between the core and other activity centers.

On-Street Parking

Although generally it is desirable for on-street parking to be available for the convenience of short-term use, sometimes it must be eliminated to accommodate pedestrian amenities and streetscape improvements. In some cases, reducing the number of traffic lanes will make it possible to maintain on-street parking while creating a high-quality pedestrian environment.

Where angled parking lines the pedestrian spine or primary connectors, a simple switch to parallel parking can allow the widening of walkways—reducing the block's parking capacity by 20 to 30 percent, but leaving the number of traffic lanes unchanged. In any case, parallel parking is preferable in an urban setting because it improves the appearance of the street and reduces the traffic hazards associated with angled parking.

Surface Lots

Surface parking lots create gaps in the development edges that otherwise provide spatial enclosure to the streets, as well as interrupt the activities that make the street a vital and interesting place for people. Expanses of pavement and parked cars create a visually harsh environment that harms the image of the central area.

When needed, surface parking lots should be located to minimize their visibility from major arterials and pedestrian-oriented streets. A perimeter landscape

Surface parking lots should be partially screened by low walls, wrought-iron railings, and landscape plantings. The perimeter treatment of this parking lot in Chicago, constructed to meet design standards established by the city, helps to maintain visual continuity along this secondary collector street.

planting of shade trees can soften or even screen them from view; a three-to-four-foot-high screen wall or hedge also may be needed to make parked cars less visible from the street. For security, however, a clear zone should be maintained —at a level between four and eight feet (1.2 to 2.4 meters) from the ground—to ensure that the interior of the parking lot remains visible from the street. Landscaped berms are not an appropriate screening technique within the central area because of the space they require and the suburban image they convey.

Standards for the design of surface parking lots should require interior plantings, including islands defined by curbs and providing space for shade trees. Standards also should be set for the level of illumination, for use of a single fixture type that matches those used throughout the central area, and for the size and placement of signs and attendant booths in commercial lots.

Parking Structures
Parking structures require less land and can be screened from view more effectively than can surface parking, but they, too,

can lower the quality of the city center. Parking structures should not be located on the streetfront of the retail spine. Where parking structures are located on streets serving as primary pedestrian connectors, retail space should occupy at least 75 percent of the ground-level frontage to minimize interruptions in pedestrian interest and activity. On other streets where a parking structure's ground level will be occupied by cars, a landscaped setback should be employed to soften the visual impact on the street and the walkway.

The landscape treatment softened the exterior of this parking facility in Fort Lauderdale, but the scale of the garage dominates the public realm and other buildings in the area. Many cities require that garages be built within buildings rather than open directly onto the street.

One of the best examples of internal block parking is this large, multilevel parking facility in Princeton, New Jersey, which was built in the center of the block, leaving a zone 60 feet (18 meters) wide for office and residential development. The four-story buildings completely enclose the parking, enhancing adjoining properties in the city center.

Some cities have found success building parking structures on the interior of the block, providing space for multistory development on the street frontage. Development of such interior-block parking should be encouraged because it allows introduction of the active uses along pedestrian-oriented streets.

Scale is a major factor in determining how a parking structure will affect the urban environment. The length of a parking structure's exposure on any given street should be held to no more than 250 to 300 feet (76 to 91 meters), with a width of 180 feet (55 meters)—three bays of parking—preferred.

The architecture of the parking structure should incorporate exterior finish materials of the same quality as those used on nearby buildings, with neutral colors and architectural forms that echo the characteristics of adjacent buildings. The street facade of the parking structure should be designed to replicate the fenestration patterns of nearby buildings to help the structure blend into the core's architectural fabric. In no case should the design of a parking structure draw attention to itself through the use of exotic shapes, materials, or colors.

Security concerns, perhaps more in terms of perception than actual crime levels, can discourage the use of parking structures. Open or glass-enclosed stairwells, glass-enclosed elevators, and even higher levels of illumination can enhance the psychological comfort felt by users. In sensitive locations (i.e., adjacent to residential uses), care should be taken to shield neighboring areas from garage lights.

Commercial space at street level of the parking facility in Princeton is occupied by neighborhood retail stores and services supported by the people who live and work in the city's central area. Walkway and streetscape improvements provide an ideal environment for residents attracted to this city center development.

Parking structures that are an integral part of a principal-use building can present even more difficult design problems than freestanding parking decks. A high-rise tower that rises from a parking podium is considered the least desirable design solution; this arrangement tends to weaken the building's relationship to the street and to create an inhospitable ground-level environment.

Underground parking has the least visual impact on the central area and creates only minimal impacts on the pedestrian environment, but it is also the most expensive option—approximately twice the cost of an above-grade parking structure. Nevertheless, the additional money spent for underground parking may be appropriate if the proposed development can support the additional construction cost. The development of underground parking by public/private ventures (e.g., Post Office Square in Boston) has demonstrated the economic benefits of subsurface parking facilities constructed in conjunction with major open-space amenities.

The high cost of land in many cities has forced developers and parking authorities to construct parking facilities under buildings or under adjacent parks and plazas. Examples illustrating how high-quality space can be created above subsurface parking include (from top): Post Office Square Park in Boston; Toronto-Dominion Centre in Toronto, Canada; and Mellon Square plaza in Pittsburgh, Pennsylvania.

117

There is only meager evidence that we recognize the urgent task confronting us—to shift the emphasis from "bigger" to "better," from the quantitative to the qualitative, and to give significant form and beauty to our environment.

CHAPTER 11

Development Guidelines

The buildings that frame the city center's streets and public spaces influence both the visual character and the vitality of the pedestrian environment. These buildings must relate positively to the street and to one another to provide the city center with visual coherence, a clear organizing structure, and a high degree of functional integration. Analysis of the existing architecture will identify the common characteristics in building placement and design that contribute to the image and sense of pedestrian orientation. This understanding of the context is the starting point for the renovation of buildings and the placement and design of new structures.

The important contributions that architecture can make to the city center environment include the following:

❖ *Establishing a continuous developed edge along streets that serve as primary paths of movement to create a coherent, unified urban structure.* Buildings form the walls that give clear definition to the street space. Consistent building setbacks and orientation to the street reinforce the perception of the street as a defined space. Infill development that repairs gaps in the urban fabric is crucial, especially on major pedestrian and arterial streets.

Eighth Street, Holland, Michigan.

or regional vocabulary of architectural forms and materials rather than allow anonymous, noncontextual architecture to weaken the city's special identity.

❖ *Creating a sense of human scale, activity, and interest at the street level to enhance the appeal of the city center to pedestrians and to promote the integration of individual projects and development blocks.* Zoning regulations, development codes, and incentives should be established to bring street-level uses to the edge of the pedestrian zone. Lower-story facades should be designed to share activity inside buildings with the street through the use of large windows and on-street entrances. Activity can even spill over into the street environment, as occurs with outdoor seating for restaurants and cafés.

It is not necessary to control the design details of new or renovated buildings to achieve coherent development. However, it is necessary that basic decisions be coordinated on setbacks, heights, cornice lines, overall facade organization, materials, ground-level programming, and storefront design.

Renovation and Reuse

The human scale, high-quality materials, and architectural detailing of older buildings add interest and identity to the environment. Wherever possible, examples of the city center's traditional commercial, civic, and residential architecture should be preserved, renovated and, where appropriate, adapted for new uses. Once-obsolete industrial buildings are finding a

Renovation of facades and storefronts in Charleston, South Carolina, was accomplished by design professionals working in collaboration with private property owners (above). The commercial storefronts, business signs, and streetscape in Fort Worth, Texas, contribute to creation of a special sense of place (below). Storefronts that convey openness allow people to share in the activity occurring within the shops, thus creating a livelier street environment.

❖ *Creating visual continuity through similarities in building height, scale, massing, overall organization of the facade, and use of materials, colors, and roof shapes.* The repetition of design elements or themes helps a city center to build a recognizable identity and sense of place, making it a more marketable and attractive location. This does not mean that all buildings need to look alike or that all details or materials need to come from a limited palette, but it is important to emphasize the common characteristics that make the existing architecture special. One effective way to do this is to develop or restore a local

Renovation and adaptive use of historic buildings in Charleston created a positive climate for reinvestment and regeneration by strengthening the city center's market appeal. New specialty retail, hotel, and residential development has added to the appeal of the historic district, which has become a national and international visitor destination.

new life with other uses such as offices, residential units, and retail space.

Identity and Market Appeal

The renovation and adaptive use of attractive, historic buildings helps create a positive climate for reinvestment and regeneration by strengthening the city center's market appeal. Renovation of deteriorated buildings, vacant or poorly modernized storefronts, and outdated or unattractive signs also helps a city center to overcome any image it may present of neglect and decline. While the presence of neglected buildings is a symptom of and contributing factor to economic decline, renovation of a highly visible older building can spark regeneration momentum and create an image of change and renewal, even if its direct contribution to the tax and employment base is minor.

Renovation of the shops and storefronts in Holland, Michigan, resulted from a visionary local business leader's belief that people would return to shop in the city center if the historic buildings were renovated for new retail tenants. Detailed architectural drawings were prepared for each building on the main retail street to spark interest in the effort.

Development of high-rise buildings in historic districts can lower property values and the quality of the public realm. The high-rise office buildings in Fort Worth are out of scale with the preserved and restored historic structures and streetscape.

The new commercial infill development in Charleston reflects the city's commitment to height limitations in the historic district. The four-story buildings were designed to respect the scale and architectural context of the area's older structures.

Conservation Strategies

In cities where pressures for city center development are accelerating, the preservation of older structures can play an important role in maintaining a city's distinctive identity and a sense of history and human scale. Indeed, many significant historic buildings offer special investment opportunities that may deserve particular attention and support.

A number of strategies and controls have been used to protect buildings that contribute to the historic character and architectural identity of city centers. Where redevelopment pressures are strong, these special measures are often crucial to preventing unnecessary destruction of such resources. Those responsible for managing city center development should consider the following guidelines:

❖ Existing zoning regulations should be carefully reviewed to identify areas where an increase in density is likely to create redevelopment pressures that threaten historic resources. A low-rise historic structure in an area zoned for high-rise development can be a valuable community asset.

❖ Where preservation and reuse are a priority, the designation of historic landmarks and districts can temper redevelopment pressures by requiring the review and approval of applications for demolition permits. Such designations also provide an effective mechanism for instituting the review processes needed to ensure coordination of changes to a building's architecture.

❖ Financial incentives and assistance, including tax credits and low-interest loans, will encourage investment in the preservation and rehabilitation of older and historic buildings.

❖ In some instances, public purchase is necessary to preserve historic buildings, with resale or long-term lease costs reduced to make renovation and reuse economically feasible for new owners and users.

❖ The transfer of development rights to another sector of the city can facilitate preservation of historic buildings in

areas zoned for higher-density development.

Preservation and renovation of existing buildings may not always be appropriate. Focused conservation efforts can best be defined on the basis of an architectural survey that identifies significant and contributing historic structures.

Such buildings often are concentrated in the traditional retail and commercial core, especially along principal shopping streets and in inner-city neighborhoods. Noncontributing structures in the core may provide areas for growth and new construction. Encouraging both new development and preservation can create investment opportunities, bolstering the city center's economic role in the region.

It also is important to determine when it does not make economic sense to renovate significant older buildings. This determination requires objective appraisal of a building's historical significance and economic feasibility. When a vacant older structure cannot be restored and puts a damper on interest in reinvestment in the adjacent area, demolition may be the best solution. Following a reasonable time frame for the solicitation of proposals for reuse, the public sector must be ready to take decisive action

that may result in demolition of buildings if no feasible proposals are received.

Renovation Guidelines

Guidelines for exterior renovation can be used to coordinate individual efforts to create a positive city center image and a high-quality pedestrian environment. These guidelines also can be used as an educational tool to promote private reinvestment. The first step in the process of preparing renovation guidelines is to develop a shared understanding of the design characteristics of the existing architecture and of the general principles for renovation success. These guidelines, along with other design standards, should be adopted by the city and enforced and implemented by an architectural review board.

A shared understanding of the context and community goals provides a better foundation upon which to build positive strategies for city center regeneration. Basic principles for the renovation of commercial buildings include the following:

❖ Strengthen the architectural integrity and design unity of individual facades;

❖ Create storefronts that add interest, activity, and comfort to the street environment; and

The most effective way to communicate renovation potential is to prepare a perspective sketch that illustrates the proposed improvements to the building facades and storefronts. Property owners, merchants, and city officials can be motivated to invest in building renovation if they can visualize the results of the proposed improvements. This sketch was prepared for Westminster, Maryland, to promote revitalization on Main Street.

❖ Emphasize compatibility in design, materials, and colors to make adjacent buildings appear to the viewer as one unit.

To create a unified blockface and organize the diversity of architectural styles and details on a given street, there must be an understanding of the building facade's design framework. The framework is composed of two major elements: the upper facade and the storefront.

The Upper Facade

The upper facade consists of the cornice and fascia that cap the building front, the building's upper stories, the windows that give articulation and interest to the upper architecture, and the piers that extend to ground level, support the facade visually, and frame the storefront.

The massive, solid architecture of the upper facade gives the building substance, architectural quality, and character. As a result, the design treatment, materials, and condition of the upper facade play an important role in defining the architectural style and establishing a relationship among buildings within the block.

Cornice and Fascia. A cornice or fascia creates a strong roofline and gives a finished appearance to the building facade. If these elements have been removed or built over, they should be restored to reemphasize the original design intent of the structure. The new cornice or fascia should be designed in proportion to the overall mass of the building.

Wall Materials. Original wall materials should be cleaned and repaired, and all exposed mechanical equipment, unused electrical apparatuses, or sign supports removed. Wherever possible, applied surface materials such as metal paneling, tile, and stucco also should be removed and the building's original wall surface and detailing restored. Special attention should be given to the removal of storefront surface materials that extend onto the piers and walls of the upper facade: such applied treatments may affect the integrity of the original architecture and weaken the balance between these two principal facade components. If new materials and colors are to be applied, they should be selected to coordinate with neighboring structures and to complement the design of the storefront. Such changes should be limited to buildings with surfaces that cannot be restored or where facades are architecturally undistinguishable.

The windows and piers in the upper facade give articulation and interest to the restored office buildings in Bethesda, Maryland, and colorful banners and storefront signs enhance the pedestrian environment. The renovation and reuse of these historic buildings has contributed to the economic revival of a multiblock retail district in the city.

The quality and character of this historic street in Nuremberg, Germany, evolved from the preservation and restoration of the stone facades, the upper-story windows, and the unique architecture of the storefronts. On the opposite side of the street, the sidewalk was widened to provide space for pedestrian activities and for viewing the city's architectural history.

Windows. Original upper-story windows should be restored to create a sense of scale and to add articulation and visual interest to the upper facade. The reintroduction or reglazing of the facade's original upper-story windows will produce a dramatic effect on the architectural integrity of many commercial buildings. The proportions of the restored windows and the rhythm of the window pattern should replicate the original facade design as closely as possible.

Piers. The piers, which frame the storefront and visually anchor the upper facade, play an essential role in creating the unified architectural framework that organizes the street level's visual diversity. Where piers have been eliminated or reduced in size, the architectural definition of the ground-level facade may be weakened and the upper architecture inadequately balanced. If this is the case, the width and spacing of the piers should be restored to give support to the facade. Piers that segment the storefront are recommended on wide buildings to improve proportional balance. To emphasize the integral role piers play in defining the architectural character of the upper facade, they should be treated with the same surface material as the facade.

Storefronts and upper facades are framed by masonry piers, which play an essential role in creating a unified street environment. Piers also help to organize the visual diversity that occurs at street level. Lowell, Massachusetts, was one of the first cities in the United States to discover and renovate its historic resources.

activity that make the street interesting and inviting. Storefronts act as unifying elements within the blockface by creating strong horizontal connections, including continuous display windows, a consistent sign frieze, and colorful awnings that link buildings together.

The storefront is the focus of the facade, providing visual interest and a sense of activity that make the street interesting and inviting. These storefronts in San Francisco act as a unifying element within the blockface by creating strong horizontal connections, including continuous display windows and colorful awnings that link buildings.

The Storefront

The street-level storefront is defined by the upper facade's piers and the sign frieze that separates the storefront's display windows and entrance from the upper architecture. This lower portion of the facade provides visual and physical access to the business located within and is the area in which the individuality and identity of that business can best be expressed. It is also the area seen and experienced most directly by pedestrians.

The storefront is the focus of the facade, providing the visual interest and sense of

Display Windows. Renovation of the lower facade should emphasize the open character of the storefront and its contribution to the street. The amount of window exposure in the area framed by the sign frieze and the piers of the upper facade should be maximized. The storefront should read as an open area and provide an active visual focus that contrasts with the solid mass of the upper facade. A continuous band of storefront display windows and entrances at street level will help to enliven the street environment and will provide an important unifying element within the blockface. Display windows should never be filled

Display windows should emphasize the open character of the storefront and its contribution to the street. A continuous band of storefront windows and entrances at street level will help enliven the street environment. The merchants in Luxembourg also use the walkway in front of their stores to sell their merchandise.

or covered, and those that have been altered should be restored to their original dimensions. Reflective glass or darkened windows should be avoided.

Entrances. Entrances are the focal points of the storefront. On more traditional buildings, recessed entrances give greater definition to the storefront, add architectural variety for pedestrians, and provide overhead protection. Where entrances are flush with the display windows, awnings can be used to create variety. Entrance doors should include glass panels that maximize the visibility of the store interior. The style of the door and its hardware should be compatible with the design character of the commercial storefront; in all cases, the use of stock residential doors should be avoided. Where entrances to upper stories are located adjacent to the storefront, they should blend into the framing architecture so that they read as secondary elements.

Awnings. An awning is a simple, inexpensive, but highly effective tool for improving the retail facade and creating a positive image for the store whose entrance it marks. Awnings provide a vehicle for introducing color, variety, and interest to the streetscape and add to the comfort of pedestrians by providing overhead protection from sun and rain. They should be used to focus attention on the storefront and create a strong horizontal element repeated along the blockface, and should be attached directly to the building without supporting columns or poles on the walkway. Hotels, theaters, and other important buildings may introduce architectural canopies to enhance their entrance or pro-

vide protection from the weather. Design guidelines should recommend an appropriate mix of awnings, canopies, and signs to maintain pedestrian scale along the street.

Side and Rear Elevations

When visible from the street or other public areas, the side and rear elevations of buildings can have a significant impact on the city center's visual character and image. While many of these exposed elevations lack the high-quality design and finish of the front facade, they can be improved to present a more attractive and organized appearance.

Corner Buildings. Because corner buildings set the tone for an entire block, their

On more traditional buildings, recessed entrances give greater definition to the storefront and add architectural variety and interest to the street facade. The awnings on the retail stores in Bethlehem, Pennsylvania, provide a means for introducing color, variety, and interest in the streetscape.

This corner building in Alexandria, Virginia, was designed to connect the retail frontage on two important streets and to provide a new entrance arcade to riverfront restaurants and open space.

127

storefronts must turn the corner to maintain streetscape continuity. On corner buildings, the original design of side elevations facing the street usually replicates the architecture of the front facade, with the side facade often creating the transition from one district of the city center to another. The same guidelines for maintaining or restoring the storefront and upper floors of the main facade should be applied to side elevations.

Unfinished Side Elevations. Where unfinished side elevations are visible from the street, they should be upgraded through the removal or screening of exposed mechanical equipment and extension of the front facade's wall materials, color, or detailing. Where windows cannot be introduced, painted graphics applied to unbroken wall surfaces can add interest. Graphics usually are most effective when contained within an area of neutral color.

Rear Elevations. When parking is located behind city center buildings, rear elevations become important secondary entrances. They should be designed to be inviting and to create an identity related to the front facade. At a minimum, all wall surfaces should be clean and in good repair. Service and storage areas should be organized, well screened, and carefully maintained. Blocked windows should be reopened; an attractive entrance door, a business sign, and lighting should be added to give the rear facade customer appeal. Awnings, display windows, and landscaping also can enhance rear elevations.

Signs

As elements of commercial architecture, signs have a big impact on the quality and appearance of individual buildings and on the streetscape as a whole. Signs can be designed and located to complement building architecture, but too often they are a major contributor to visual chaos along the street.

Signs are used to identify a business, create its image, and indicate the goods and services it offers. To be successful, a sign must be eye-catching and make its point without providing too many details or using too many words, while at the same time not be so abstract that its message is ambiguous. Each sign should complement the architecture of the building on which it is located and serve as a unifying element in the blockface.

Graphic simplicity and compatibility with the building architecture are the basic principles of designing an effective and attractive system of signs. The sign's components—size, location, materials, color, lettering, and illumination—can help both to create a positive identity for an individual business and to provide a unified image for the city center.

Size. The size of each sign should be proportional to the scale of the storefront and the building facade as a whole; signs should never obscure or overwhelm the basic architectural character of the building. A ratio of one square foot of sign area for each linear foot of building frontage is a good rule of thumb to use in determining the appropriate size of facade signs. Projecting signs should not exceed 20 square feet (1.9 square meters).

Location. On traditional multistory commercial buildings, signs fit most naturally on the lintel or sign frieze that separates the ground-level storefront from the upper facade. In this location, the sign serves as a boundary between the two major facade components and helps strengthen their definition. Wherever possible, signs on separate businesses sharing the blockface should be located at about the same height to create a unifying element.

Materials. The major consideration in selecting sign materials is compatibility

with the building's overall architectural character. Many materials are appropriate, including wood, metal, plastic, neon, and canvas. Materials that convey an image of low quality, such as plastic panel, should be avoided.

Color. Graphic design and use of color can enhance the pedestrian experience of walking along streets in the retail district. While bright colors are entirely appropriate for signs, too many colors can be confusing.

The small projecting signs on King Street in Alexandria complement the buildings to which they are attached and serve as a unifying element on the blockface.

The merchants in Quebec City, Canada, have employed graphic artists to design hundreds of colorful business signs to enliven the street environment.

129

Message. The words on a sign should be limited to the name of the business and other pertinent information related to its operation. The sign should never be used for product advertising. Simplicity is the key to legibility and elegance: bold, simple lettering styles and the use of recognized symbols are most effective.

Illumination. Signs that flash or move are generally inappropriate for the city center; indirectly lit signs are preferred. Most storefront signs can be illuminated by the streetlights located in the pedestrian amenity zone.

Lighting of civic buildings and monuments can add to the ambience of the city center. Private developers and their architects should consider special facade lighting to enhance the total public realm.

New Development

New development should be designed to complement the existing architecture and reinforce its features.

Infill Development

Infill development can repair and strengthen the urban fabric by eliminating gaps created by vacant lots and surface parking. After protection of high-quality, existing architecture, introduction of such infill should be the primary development priority. The pedestrian spine, primary connectors, transit streets, and major arterial streets should be the key target locations for infill development.

Infill buildings must be sensitively designed to reinforce the positive characteristics of the existing architecture.

This new office building in Alexandria was designed to reinforce the positive characteristics of the existing architecture. The objective of contextual design is to translate the fundamental qualities of existing development into contemporary buildings that use 21st-century technology and building materials.

A blend of old and new buildings can add variety, interest, and depth to the city center's visual character. In Washington, D.C., many historic structures are being restored and incorporated into the fabric of the new office and residential buildings. The infill buildings must be sensitively designed to complement the scale and architectural character of the historic structures.

Contextual design is not application of a period architectural style to a new building. Instead, its objective is to translate fundamental design characteristics of existing development into a compatible contemporary idiom.

Under the conditions in which the pre-20th century traditional marketplace developed, basic building scale, forms, orientation, and materials were relatively consistent. Variety and contrast were provided primarily by differences in detail and ornamentation at a relatively minor scale. As a result, overall consistency and continuity were easy to achieve.

However, technological innovations—e.g., the elevator, air conditioning, steel-frame construction—and modern architecture allowed and encouraged a greater range of choice in building form, scale, materials, and character. Consequently, the potential for contrast became much greater. In trying to create a distinctive identity for a particular project, newer urban architecture has tended to ignore consistency in favor of dramatic contrasts. Often, this extreme variety creates disorder and a lack of harmony in the urban environment.

A blend of old and new buildings can add variety, interest, and depth to the city center's visual character. Similarly, sharp contrasts in building design can be exciting and dramatic when they create meaningful focal points and landmarks. But to be effective, contrasting buildings must be set within a relatively uniform and quiet architectural context. It also is important to note that the tolerance for contrast decreases in direct proportion with city size: in smaller cities, sharp contrasts must be introduced carefully to avoid destroying the existing architectural order.

If infill buildings are to be compatible with existing development, they must emulate—rather than imitate—key aspects of existing development. Each block and each street will have its own vocabulary. The following guidelines provide some clues on how to maintain a consistent design vocabulary.

Front Setbacks. New development should replicate the setbacks of existing buildings to create a consistent developed edge, reinforce the city center's urban development pattern, and enhance pedestrian orientation. In the central core, existing setbacks usually coincide with the right-of-way line, making it possible for active ground-level uses to open directly onto the pedestrian zone.

Spacing between Buildings. Side-yard setbacks should echo the rhythm of spacing between existing buildings. In the more intensively developed urban core, side-yard setbacks are usually eliminated, except where through-block pedestrian walkways are provided.

131

Building Height and Massing.
Height and massing should be compatible with existing development, with sensitive transitions in height provided between existing low-rise development and taller new structures. The building mass should be broken into increments that correspond to the scale and massing of existing buildings through the use of setbacks and variable roof heights.

Building Entrances.
The major building facade and entrance should be oriented toward streets that are designated as the pedestrian spine, primary connectors, or major arterials. The spacing and articulation of entrances should replicate those of existing buildings.

Facade Organization.
As is the case with traditional commercial architecture, the street facades of new infill development should be organized into two major components, the ground-level storefront and the upper architecture, with strong horizontal elements separating the two. Especially on pedestrian streets, where a sense of human scale and amenities are essential, the ground-level storefronts should provide large window areas to share the building's interior activities with the street. If structured parking is part of the building, these street frontage spaces should never be occupied by parking.

Major New Development

The principal challenge in designing major city center development projects is to incorporate large-scale and high-rise structures into the existing context of smaller-scale buildings. On a street or in a district where an attractive and consistent architectural character exists, an appropriate degree of compatibility is important. The dominant scale and setbacks of existing buildings should establish the framework into which new architecture fits. When the existing architecture is mediocre, however, the first new project can establish the baseline on which other new buildings can build to create a new context. Certainly, where the existing standard of design is poor, the repetition of design elements is not desirable, and new development should be used to set a new standard.

In new larger-scale developments, buildings should be broken into smaller units that complement the existing urban fabric and provide transitions in height and

scale; unarticulated forms and masses should be avoided. Multiblock mega-structures can harm the center city by destroying the street grid, the basic organizing structure, and the efficient flow of pedestrians.

Setting Appropriate Height Limits. To determine the appropriate maximum height for new development, the goals of the city center development should first be considered. Among the considerations are the following:

❖ which is desired in a particular area—rehabilitation of existing structures or redevelopment—and whether effective means can be established to protect significant structures or districts;

❖ the priority that should be given to spreading market potential horizontally to create a high-quality street environment;

❖ development economics affected by such factors as the disparity between existing and permitted development densities, the influence of land cost on development feasibility, and the market's ability to absorb a large amount of additional leasable space in a reasonable time frame;

❖ the ability of the development to accommodate increased traffic and parking demands without lowering the quality of the street-level environment; and

❖ the way guidelines for the placement of high-rise buildings will be applied in order to minimize the development's visual, shadow, and wind impacts.

If these objective considerations fail to point to an appropriate building height, a decision on the issue becomes more subjective and political. But the decision still will be influenced by the desire to balance economic development and land planning objectives—that is, increased employment and tax revenues and the creation of a critical mass of activity in a compact core—with the objective of creating a desirable community identity and maintaining human scale. No one right answer exists, but it should not be forgotten that the design treatment of the street level is just as important as the height of the buildings in establishing the image of the city center.

Locating High Rises. Where the city center's existing architecture creates a desirable identity and a human scale on the pedestrian spine and primary connector streets, it usually is best to maintain

High-rise buildings constructed around Copley Square in Boston dominate Trinity Church and the historic buildings in the Back Bay area (left). In Oakland, California, developers were required to provide additional open space to obtain zoning approval for development of a high-rise office complex in the city center (right).

133

Parks and open space in Sydney, Australia, provide an excellent setting for the high-rise buildings in the city center. High-rise development should be encouraged in areas of the city where adequate open space is available or where it can be created over time.

the traditional architectural image on principal street frontages and to add higher-density, high-rise buildings either at midblock or at locations bordering the traditional core. In either case, new higher-density buildings should be within easy walking distance of traditional retail concentrations to reinforce the central area's economic vitality rather than create a competing activity center.

Transitions in building height and mass must be carefully designed. City-mandated height-to-setback ratios, for example, can minimize the visibility of the high-rise building from the traditional street frontage.

Countering High-Rise Impacts.

It is possible to counter the psychological effects of the upward thrust of a high-rise facade by creating a strong horizontal element that establishes a "ceiling" for the street. Lintels or setbacks, which define the effective height of the facade as perceived at street level, should be located at the height of cornice lines or lintels of existing buildings.

Materials and forms that provide a scale of reference and a sense of three-dimensional articulation at ground level can help a development, including a high-rise building, retain a sense of human scale at street

level. The use of reflective glass at ground level should be avoided so that the building base will meet the ground in a manner that humanizes the street environment. To increase the visual appeal of high-rise buildings on the skyline, sculpting of the top of the high-rise tower can be required by city codes. Also, codes designed to allow the sun to reach streets and public spaces, and measures that help to minimize wind-tunnel and downdraft effects, should be adopted.

Megastructures.

Developments, whether low-rise, high-rise, or a combination of building heights that take up a full block or span several blocks—such as a new retail center or major mixed-use development—are known as megastructures. Special care is required to integrate such large-scale developments into their surroundings. When these projects span several blocks, they can disrupt the original street grid that gives the city center a consistent development pattern and cut off street-level linkages between key locations. Megastructures must be designed to maintain pedestrian connections and view corridors and to share their internal activity with the street. Architecture that creates buildings that turn their back to the city, present blank walls to the perimeter streets, or internalize all their activity should be avoided. Recommendations for minimizing these negative impacts include the following:

❖ Incorporate existing buildings and/or facades into megacomplexes;

❖ Break the horizontal expanse of long facades into smaller increments that relate to the traditional human scale of city center streets through the use of windows, architectural detailing, variable setbacks, and rooflines;

❖ Articulate the building mass as an aggregation of smaller components to reduce the perception of overwhelming bulk;

❖ Provide a sequence of public spaces and walkways that are linked to the street grid;

❖ Orient major facades and entrances toward the streets that serve as important pedestrian corridors;

❖ Use ground-floor storefronts and retail activity to integrate the structure functionally with the street; and

❖ Design transitions between the height and massing of the megaproject and existing or planned neighboring structures.

Established guidelines for such new construction or adaptive use enable developers to understand clearly the community's objectives for creating a more coherent pattern of development and a more attractive environment. Required adherence to such guidelines will eliminate prolonged disputes about new proposals and raise the overall quality of design while allowing considerable architectural freedom. The objective of such guidelines is not to stifle investment and innovation, but to ensure that development of megaprojects does not occur at the expense of the overall character and the future prospects of the city center at large.

Special care is required to integrate large-scale development into the city's existing fabric of streets and open space. Megastructures must be designed to maintain pedestrian connections and view corridors and to share their internal activities with the street. The retail shops in this Philadelphia center should be reoriented to the street to activate this important image corridor.

The streetscape, plazas, and green space on the Chicago lakefront create a high-quality environment for high-density residential development on North Michigan Avenue. New infill development is controlled by design standards established by the city.

To build a better city is to work at the heart of civilization.

—Mort Hoppenfeld

CHAPTER 12

Planning Guidelines

The successful city center should provide the region with a desirable range of uses while demonstrating economic potential and development feasibility. To recruit potential developers and tenants, the development community and city officials need to act as entrepreneurs, ready to provide existing and potential businesses and residents with political support and financial assistance.

Long-, intermediate-, and short-term planning must be coordinated and logically connected. Too often, short-term expediency—immersion in current problems, acceptance of any and all development proposals, lack of available resources, fear of any change—stunts a more far-reaching yet feasible vision. Because of staff limitations, cities may need outside expertise to help them devise and implement planning strategies that are responsive to market conditions. The guidelines outlined here can serve as a checklist in preparing these strategies.

Bartlett Square, Tulsa, Oklahoma.

Identify Issues and Opportunities

❖ *Study the experiences of other cities.* Although each city center is unique in its market conditions and development potential, a broad understanding of the things other cities have achieved and how they have achieved them can provide a significant head start. While it is important to guard against the dangers of imitative solutions, understanding the process other cities have gone through to improve their situation may be of great value in establishing a strategy for the city center.

❖ *Evaluate the strengths and weaknesses of the local market.* To avoid wasted time and effort, it is essential to understand why desirable market components are missing and to identify early targets for strengthening the city center's mix. In general, office, cultural, institutional, and entertainment uses, including restaurants, are the best early targets. Housing also may have early potential. It is important to seek expert assistance in evaluating local market opportunities and strategies for transforming proposals into viable projects.

❖ *Envision the future image of the city center.* Even if market analysis shows little or no demand for a given use based on existing conditions and a projection of current trends, a change in the city center's image and environment can create a demand or market where none previously existed. A series of "what if" scenario exercises may uncover hidden potential.

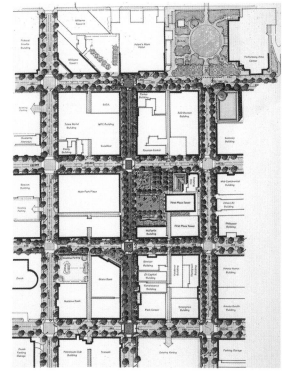

Public officials need to have a clearly defined physical plan and vision to guide and direct development in the city center. In Tulsa, the private sector, in partnership with the city, prepared a detailed design plan for public realm improvements in the central core and an urban design concept for future development of the underused areas adjacent to the city center.

The two most important retail streets in Tulsa were closed to vehicular traffic in the 1970s to provide additional space for pedestrians. Over time, the retail stores departed and the office tenants moved to more accessible locations.

When the decision was made to reopen the streets, plans and sketches were prepared to illustrate how the pedestrian space at the intersection of Main and Fifth streets would be redesigned to accommodate limited vehicular traffic.

❖ *Conduct an inventory of physical assets.* This will suggest opportunities for strengthening market potential and broadening the base of city center uses, as will an identification of disincentives and barriers to development and alternative solutions.

Ensure Broad-Based Participation and Consensus Building

❖ *Encourage stakeholder participation and frequent public outreach.* Include in the planning process all who have a vested interest in the city center—existing businesses, residents, building owners, developers, city agencies, and other institutions. The broadest possible participation in framing issues and objectives should be encouraged.

❖ *Establish a public/private partnership.* Mobilize the expertise and resources of the community's business leaders to define issues and implement solutions through public/private partnership organizations. Any partnership should place private sector leadership in a

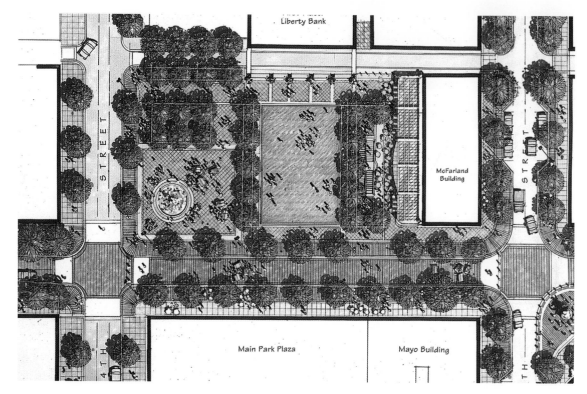

Liberty Bank

McFarland
Building

Main Park Plaza

Mayo Building

STREET

4 TH

A new fountain plaza and green space are being constructed in Tulsa to generate pedestrian activity along Main Street. A bank building and a restaurant will open onto the fountain plaza and Main Street, adding life and vitality to this important commercial street in the city center.

strong management position with an executive director and staff to implement the program.

❖ *Use a cooperative, consensus-based process for decision making.* Emphasize informal decision-making structures.

❖ *Go slowly to go fast.* Invest the necessary time in the beginning to define issues, objectives, and values; do not get bogged down in detailed solutions before a consensus is reached on a clearly defined vision.

❖ *Make the process of finding solutions open, collaborative, and educational.* People who are expected to object to plans can be made part of the solution if they are involved in the planning process. Review the experiences of other cities; call in a variety of experts.

❖ *Work toward buy-in by all sectors of the stakeholder group.* Achieve a consensus

on goals and strategies to gain support for the public financial assistance that is necessary to make the city center retail and residential development feasible to the private sector.

Develop Planning Products

❖ *Bring the vision to life.* Use models, sketches, and photo simulations based on supportive planning analysis to communicate the urban design objectives.

❖ *Emphasize issue-specific, implementation-oriented programs and projects.*

❖ *Establish a clear framework for achieving longer-term goals and coordinating changes in the city center's physical structure.*

❖ *Identify projects that can generate early tangible results.* This will mobilize community commitment and support, build

The open space in front of this Tulsa office tower was not designed to accommodate major public functions, and the dense planting of trees on Main Street limited views of this important area.

confidence, and project an image of renewal. Focus early efforts on what is most achievable.

❖ *Use improvements to the public environment as a catalyst for private initiatives.*

❖ *Stress a smaller-scale, incremental approach.* Do not rely on the success of one large project unless that project can be achieved within a reasonable time frame.

❖ *Be specific about short-term actions and priorities.* Keep longer-term initiatives more general, but define a clear, organizing physical framework to coordinate and integrate public and private investments.

❖ *Use the overall plan as a promotional tool.* Identify private sector development and investment opportunities, communicate those opportunities, and sell the merits of the plan and implementation strategy to the community and business leaders.

The image and vision for Tulsa's fountain plaza and the Main Street improvements were communicated through the use of this perspective sketch. Creating a visual image of the proposed plan was an important part of the planning process and was invaluable in building consensus for the proposed public realm improvements.

141

The raised planting islands in the middle of Tulsa's Main Street limited views of the retail shops, restricted the use of space for special events, and discouraged pedestrian activity in the evening. Redesign of the street right-of-way for vehicular traffic has stimulated interest in renovation and reuse of the valuable commercial frontage.

Devise Public Sector Implementation Techniques

❖ *Share the risks with the private sector and act as an entrepreneur and codeveloper.* This will help to create a stronger tax base, and less effort will be required to attract economic development, to retain or attract households, and to create a positive image for the city center as a desirable place to live, work, and visit.

❖ *Increase the city center's competitiveness as an investment location through public sec-*

tor investments. These can include new anchor uses such as a performing arts center, a conference center, sports venues, or a government office building or a courthouse.

❖ *Use public improvements as a tangible demonstration of long-term public commitment to the city center environment.* Such efforts will be catalysts for private investment.

❖ *Take advantage of underused public land.*

❖ *Verify the commitment to the public realm.* Make certain that the stakeholders in the city center are prepared to provide excellent management and maintenance of the streetscape and public spaces.

❖ *Offer financial incentives.* These can include land writedowns, below-market-rate financing, tax increment financing, waivers of development fees, tax and fee abatement, and incentive zoning. Make available as many tools as possible.

❖ *Identify the decision makers in the public sector and give them responsibility.* Have them represent the city during discussions and make decisions related to new development projects.

❖ *Streamline the approval process.* Remove regulatory obstacles and revise development regulations and review processes to encourage the desired types and quality of development while protecting the integrity of historic structures.

❖ *Spell out clearly and emphatically in advance what the city needs and wants.* Provide guidelines to eliminate guesswork.

❖ *Provide guidelines that ensure consistently high-quality projects and a balanced land use mix.* This should be done whether development interest is weak or strong.

❖ *Create an environment for mixed-use development in the central area.* Do this by using a district plan, a development code, and development guidelines as decision-making criteria.

❖ *Work on a variety of fronts simultaneously.* Develop and adopt a plan with broad community support.

❖ *Understand that patience and persistence are needed.* Provide management structures for a long-term effort. Building a self-sustaining mix of city center uses is a lengthy process requiring adjustments and revisions along the way.

The most important commercial streets in Tulsa's city center were either closed to traffic or were part of a one-way street pattern that degraded the pedestrian environment. Boston Avenue, the historic office spine in the central area, has been redesigned as a two-way street with wider pedestrian walkways and streetscape amenities.

One of the major objectives of the private sector was to create incentives to build new residential space within walking distance of the Tulsa city center. This perspective sketch illustrates how new housing and a pedestrian greenway can be developed on underused land south of the central core.

143

A clear vision crafted by the decisions of a city's citizens and government leaders can meld a multiplicity of wills into positive, unified action to substantially change the character of a city.

—Edmund Bacon

CHAPTER 13

Visioning Process

Reviving a city center and then sustaining its success is a complex and lengthy endeavor. Hundreds, perhaps even thousands, of individuals will make decisions and play a role in the city center's evolution, meaning no single person or entity, no matter how powerful or committed, will control the process.

Developers must make investment decisions, but they cannot guarantee success or create the market demand for the spaces they create. Public sector agencies may regulate land use and design, but they cannot mandate the needed investments or the results they desire. Retailers can make their facades and interior spaces more attractive, but they cannot force potential customers to shop at their stores. Elected officials can promise support for the city center, but they cannot guarantee they will still be in office when the key votes and action to back them up are needed.

This reality means there will always be a degree of uncertainty in a city center's evolution. This open-endedness is a key reason to embrace and encourage creative planning and marketing, and flexibility in phasing.

Wisconsin Avenue, Milwaukee, Wisconsin.

This flexibility should not be a vehicle for uncoordinated pursuit of separate agendas or short-term expediency, but rather a means of achieving long-term success. To avoid such pitfalls, decision makers must agree on clearly defined, overarching goals, develop a consensus-building process, and broadcast a coherent, widely shared vision for the city center.

A workable vision for the city center is not merely a defined, detailed "plan." Nor is it a grab bag of everyone's pet desires or hopes. Rather, a workable vision is a set of mutually supportive goals created after sufficient consideration has been given to the major actions and expenditures needed to carry them out, and based on a shared awareness of how the main obstacles to achieving them can be overcome. All successful city centers have benefited from the dedication of sufficient energy, time, and negotiation to create a comprehensive vision that is credible, achievable, and shared by a broad spectrum of stakeholders.

Advocates of the city center must speak up and persist throughout the planning process. While neglect and planning strategies that favor suburbs and regional decentralization have put city centers under stress, stalwart voices have continued to offer a contrarian defense of the center's continued social, cultural, and economic assets. Philadelphia architect and planner Edmund Bacon, in particular, demonstrated this unwavering commitment. His work in that city offers insights into the importance of creating a city center vision.

The Bacon Philosophy

Edmund Bacon served as Philadelphia's lead planner from 1949 to 1970, a long tenure that enabled him to achieve much, including revival of Rittenhouse Square and the fostering of a new appreciation on the part of Philadelphians for the scale and organization of their city's historic open-space system. While the benefits of Bacon's approach were not realized during his tenure despite the length of his service, the city continued to be built according to this vision for almost a half century. The results have made Philadelphia's city center one of America's most dramatic urban success stories and one of its most popular places.

In his 1967 book *Design of Cities*, Bacon contends that human will can be imposed effectively on our cities so that the form they take expresses the highest aspirations of our civilization. Credited with inventing modern urban design, Bacon believes that, in his words, "building cities is one of man's greatest achievements," and that a city's physical form "is determined by decisions made by the people who live in it."

In leading Philadelphia's city center renaissance, Bacon demonstrated how a clear vision of a "design concept," crafted through the decisions of a city's residents and government leaders, could "meld a multiplicity of wills into positive, unified action on a scale large enough to substantially change the character of a city."

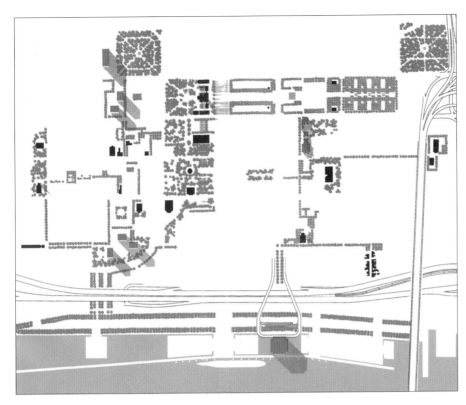

The plans, sketches, and models prepared by the Philadelphia Planning Commission inspired community leaders and private developers to invest in redevelopment of the historic district east of the city center. Edmund Bacon envisioned building a greenway system that would extend from the Delaware River to Independence Mall and the two park squares, creating the open-space amenities required to attract residents to the revitalized east side neighborhoods.

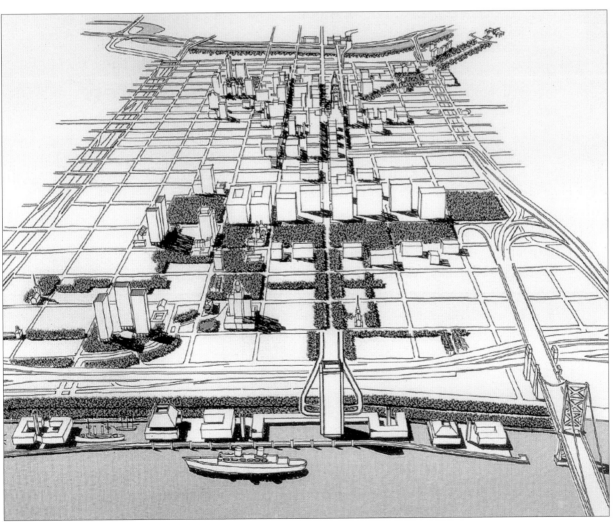

Bacon viewed city planning as a people's art—a shared experience in which policy makers, designers, residents, business owners, and community leaders play an active role in crafting a vision for their city. Through analysis, interviews, education sessions, and consensus-building exercises, these stakeholders can create a vision that not only inspires all the parties involved, but also creates a sense of ownership in the overall plan.

The role that designers and planners play in this process is to listen to the needs and desires of the community, then nurture and refine those ideas in such a way that the final product reflects the community's fundamental goals and vision. The ultimate challenge of the urban designer or planner is not just to focus on facades or architectural mass, but also to facilitate a process that inspires community decision making and action that implement the plan according to the community's priorities. The result of a successful visioning process is the graphic and verbal representation of the community's ideas—the vision of the development to come. Bacon contends, "to fail to provide a coherent vision of a finer, healthier, and more inspiring city leaves people with nothing to which they can react." The community and designer

achieve true success when they turn the process of planning and vision building into a complete, physical work of art— what Bacon terms "a city created by the interactive process produced by a plan of such clarity and form that a noble city is born."

Bacon's professional leadership and passion for design excellence inspired large and small cities throughout the United States. His faith in the visioning and consensus-building process provided community leaders and design professionals with a strategy of how to restore vitality to our cities.

The Milwaukee Visioning Process

Milwaukee, Wisconsin, offers a good recent example of the role this visioning process can play in the revitalization of a center city. In Milwaukee, the process centered on returning Wisconsin Avenue to its former prominence as a retail and commercial center and the city's most important and symbolic urban thoroughfare. While the city's focus on one street may seem narrow, the project addressed issues that affected the entire central area and that had been encountered earlier in the city's long history of city center renewal.

The Wisconsin Avenue visioning process built on a wave of city center development that took place in Milwaukee in the early and mid-1990s. By 1997, Milwaukee public officials and community leaders, realizing that such efforts needed to be better coordinated, created a partnership

Wisconsin Avenue is Milwaukee's most important commercial street and the central pedestrian spine for the entire city center. The eastern portion of Wisconsin Avenue, shown here, links the city center to the Milwaukee Art Museum and the lakefront parks and amenities.

with the Milwaukee Redevelopment Corporation, a nonprofit organization composed of leading Milwaukee businessmen, to update the city's core area plan. As part of this effort, the city and the redevelopment corporation hired A. Nelessen Associates (Team ANA) to formulate a new vision for a revitalized city center.

Public Input

The 30-month process began with interviews of stakeholders, including elected officials, business and education leaders, and neighborhood associations. Public forums also were held and community surveys were conducted to open an active dialogue about the future of central Milwaukee.

These initial discussions and intense public participation sessions provided the basis for the first concept plan, which was presented to the public for feedback. The plan was detailed enough to address the key issues and desires identified in the interviews, forums, and surveys, with appropriate infill development and the quality of the pedestrian environment topping the list.

As the design process continued, Team ANA members met with key stakeholders to refine the plan and suggest implementation strategies. Participants were asked in a visual preference survey to indicate the type and character of streets and places that they thought were appropriate

Lake Michigan

The development plan for central Milwaukee emphasized the need to improve the public realm throughout the city center. The plan that evolved from the visioning process illustrates how the streets and open space would unite to create a green infrastructure to enhance the quality of people's lives.

Two important parks located on the northern edge of the city center provide open-space amenities for people who work in the central area and for residents who live in the revitalized north side neighborhoods. Both of these public spaces were studied to determine how they could be improved to better serve the needs of the people in the community.

and acceptable—or inappropriate and unacceptable—for the city center based on its character and needs. Not surprisingly, the survey found support for wide walkways, street trees, high-quality paving, and pedestrian amenities. Overall, survey participants ranked the walking experience as the most important element in the city center plan.

Plan Recommendations

The Milwaukee Downtown Plan presented to the city in 1999 included text, images, maps, framework diagrams, and drawings.

It offered recommendations addressing infill development, building types, the pedestrian realm, wayfinding, transit, the streetscape, and neighborhood connections.

It also set clear objectives for the city to pursue and identified a number of "catalytic projects" with the greatest potential to improve Milwaukee's central area immediately. For each of these projects, the ANA team members identified the ultimate goal of the work, the benefits it would provide, the parties responsible for implementation, and the rationale behind the work. The team gave its recommendations for how each project should be pursued, and concept drawings were prepared.

One of the catalytic projects advocated by the Downtown Plan was a redesign of Wisconsin Avenue to improve the pedestrian environment and create an environment

The recommended enhancement plan for Juneau Park focused on improving the walkway system and the overlook plazas, which are designed to provide pedestrians with a place to rest and enjoy views of the lakefront parks and amenities.

that would promote continued economic development. Wisconsin Avenue is the most important pedestrian street in the city center, serving as the public entrance and the link to several developments, including the Midwest Express Convention Center, the Grand Avenue retail center, and the Milwaukee Art Museum. The Downtown Plan identified public realm improvements on this high-profile main street that would capitalize on recent investments along the corridor, recapture the avenue's former grandeur, and attract more people to the heart of the city.

For Wisconsin Avenue to fulfill its role as the city's premier destination street, extensive streetscape improvements along an 18-block stretch were required. The ANA team investigated opportunities for designing walkable spaces that would incorporate wide walkways, large street trees, and high-quality materials and amenities. However, existing conditions constrained the improvements: because hollow utility vaults beneath the walkways prohibited improvements under the existing street configuration, the walkways needed to be extended into the parking lane to accommodate street trees and pedestrian amenities, street furniture, and space for outdoor cafés and street vendors.

However, improvements to the pedestrian realm alone were not expected to be sufficient to stimulate private investment. The quality of such an environment can easily be diminished by city center traffic, especially buses. To enhance the pedestrian realm, the Downtown Plan recommended that routes for large buses be transferred from Wisconsin Avenue to two parallel streets, Wells and Michigan. The relocation of the bus routes would reduce noise and fumes and would eliminate the need to commit walkway space to bus stops. The plan also proposed introduction of small-scale electric transit shuttles, which, combined with the newly enhanced pedestrian realm, would encourage use of the Wisconsin Avenue pedestrian/ transit spine.

Completion of the Downtown Plan was the first step in providing city and private sector leaders with a workable strategy and vision for the future. Following this step, the city received federal funding from the U.S. Department of Transportation to improve its pedestrian realm and to plan a new transit connector system to facilitate internal circulation and connections to adjacent city center neighborhoods. Following the recommendations made in the Downtown Plan, the city proposed that the funds be used for the first phase of streetscape improvements on the western sector of Wisconsin Avenue.

The most intensively used open space in the city center is Cathedral Square, a small urban park popular because it is adjacent to a thriving retail and restaurant district. The park enhancement plan recommended development of a new plaza around the fountain to provide space for café tables and chairs, while the lawn would be reserved for people wanting to picnic on the grass.

The Herzfeld Foundation Studies

Concurrent with the work on a vision for Milwaukee's center city, the private Richard and Ethel Herzfeld Foundation, with the city's consent, hired LDR International, an HNTB company, to provide urban design services. The foundation and the LDR team subsequently concluded that the proposed improvements to the pedestrian realm on Wisconsin

Avenue, renovations proposed for Cathedral Square and Juneau Park, and other open-space enhancement proposals were the most important projects to implement. Consequently, the team refined the design concepts for the pedestrian realm to establish more definitive recommendations for streetscape improvements on Wisconsin Avenue.

The team's urban design plans and perspective sketches illustrated the change that would result from the redesign and enhancement of the pedestrian realm. For example, the design plan showed a way to expand the existing walkways by eight feet (2.4 meters) to provide space beyond the utility vaults for street trees and pedestrian amenities. Building on the participatory process, the team had property owners, community leaders, and city and county officials review

Creation of a wide, tree-lined boulevard will encourage people to walk the length of Wisconsin Avenue to reach the Milwaukee Art Museum and other lakefront amenities. This gateway to the city center can once again become the prestigious street that inspires and excites people who live and work in Milwaukee.

Great streets are developed by community leaders willing to be engaged in the visioning process. Often, the most important decisions regarding the urban environment are made without adequate involvement of the community. This sketch was prepared to stimulate interest in rebuilding the pedestrian realm on Wisconsin Avenue.

streetscape improvement plans for Wisconsin Avenue and enhancement proposals for two major city center parks. In turn, the recommendations from these work sessions and community meetings were incorporated into the design plans and final sketches.

These perspective sketches and design plans that evolved from the Herzfeld Foundation–supported work helped the team to refine and further articulate the objectives of the 1999 Downtown Plan. The review brought out the need to improve the Wisconsin Avenue pedestrian realm and to encourage people to walk to the retail and entertainment area west of Plankinton Avenue. It also led to recommendations to eliminate

some of the on-street parking in order to provide additional space for streetscape improvements and outdoor cafés. Also suggested was preservation of four lanes of traffic in order to accommodate the electric transit shuttles and other vehicular traffic and to provide service access for buildings fronting on Wisconsin Avenue.

Benefits and Constraints

The Milwaukee experience illustrates the benefits of the visioning process, but also shows how difficult it can be to establish consensus on key public realm projects. For example, LDR's proposal received support from the business community and most city officials, but city traffic and transportation engineers opposed narrowing the street and eliminating the on-street parking. Although it was true that under the proposal, 65 on-street parking spaces would be removed, the plan took into account the fact that there were more than 7,500 public parking spaces available within a five-minute walk of the offices and commercial development along the Wisconsin Avenue corridor.

Expanding the walkway by eight feet (2.4 meters) would provide space for street trees, pedestrian-scale lighting, and street furniture. The great historic buildings that have been renovated, along with new office buildings constructed on Wisconsin Avenue, merit development of a high-quality pedestrian environment.

As in other city centers where the value of widened walkways and enhanced pedestrian environments has been demonstrated, Milwaukee's Wisconsin Avenue has the potential to attract thousands of people every day. The Downtown Plan states, "Pedestrians are the lifeblood of the city center," and that careful design and maintenance of the pedestrian realm is critical to the enhancement of central Milwaukee. As the first step toward achieving the vision laid out in the Downtown Plan, public officials, business leaders, and community members outlined the following objectives in order to prioritize and emphasize the importance of the pedestrian realm:

❖ Replace a negative, uninviting public realm with a positive, appealing space;

❖ Create a pedestrian-friendly environment through streetscape improvements and added amenities;

❖ Create a streetwall of high-quality facades;

❖ Restore existing facades to traditional historic character;

❖ Ensure that the primary entrances to stores and offices are on Wisconsin Avenue;

❖ Program a new mix of merchandise, services, and facilities; and

❖ Introduce a smaller, cleaner, and more efficient public transit vehicle on the avenue.

Fulfillment of these objectives will transform this premier street into a visually unified, safe, and lively pedestrian corridor. By following the community's vision and plan for this central area destination, Milwaukee has the potential to make Wisconsin Avenue one of the world's great streets, and the center city as a whole would benefit tremendously from this success.

Historically, the major retail tenants anchored the west end of Wisconsin Avenue, with all the stores opening directly onto the street to create an exciting shopping environment. But development of an interior shopping arcade closed most of the storefronts and reoriented them to the interior space. This sketch illustrates the opportunity that exists to reactivate the retail frontage on Wisconsin Avenue.

A plan to develop a new outdoor activity space for special events was recommended to city officials. The convention center, the adjoining hotels, and the retail district will benefit from the creation of a special sense of place at the west end of Wisconsin Avenue.

155

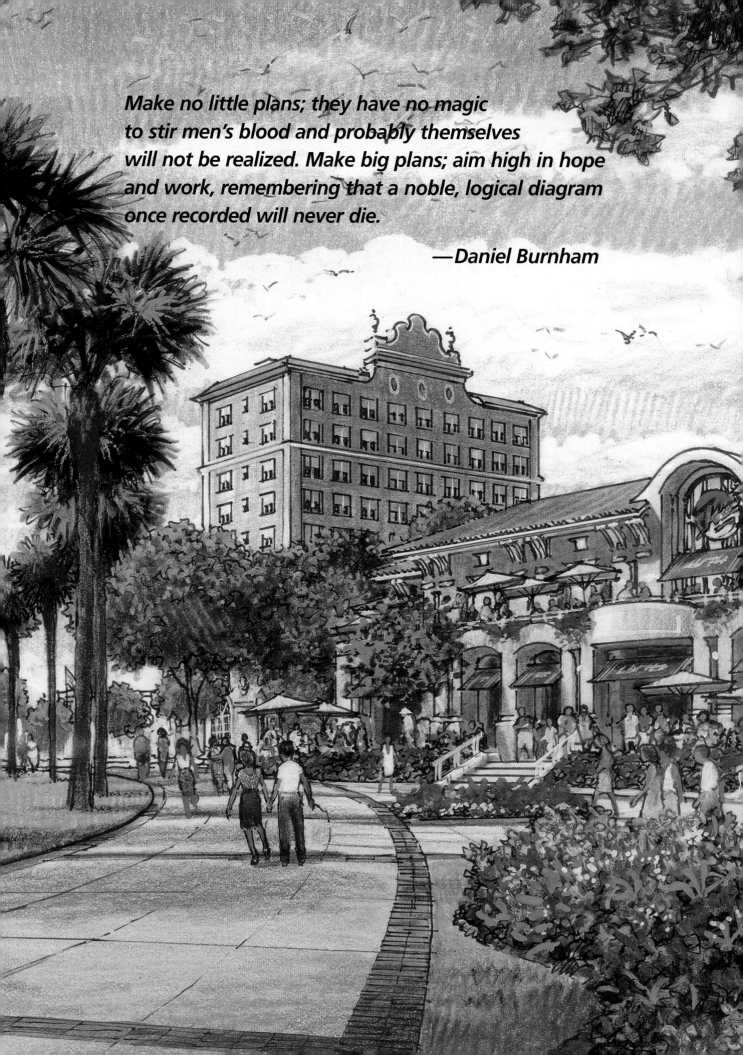

*Make no little plans; they have no magic
to stir men's blood and probably themselves
will not be realized. Make big plans; aim high in hope
and work, remembering that a noble, logical diagram
once recorded will never die.*

—*Daniel Burnham*

Development Plan

All communities need a plan for the future that sets forth concepts and strategies for improving the quality of the city center. This plan should provide a statement of policies and a list of criteria for decision making that inform developers in advance of the community's expectations and objectives for city center development. A good plan helps define the rules of the game for all the players, and, along with the tools used to implement it, provides a predictable framework for decision making and a basis for coordinating public and private investments.

The development plan is a guide for how to organize the activities of public agencies whose decisions affect the city center's future. In addition, an established plan with a list of priorities serves as an "insurance policy" for pioneering developers and investors by assuring them that their projects will be enhanced and strengthened by future development. Moreover, the plan can serve as a marketing tool by identifying development opportunities and communicating the public sector's commitment to new appropriate private investment.

Lake Mirror Park, Lakeland, Florida.

For a plan to be implemented effectively, there must be political support for and broad community consensus in favor of its objectives. The planning process must be structured to educate the public about urban design issues and principles and to gain public agreement on development guidelines. The plan itself must be oriented toward action and identify specific short-term projects that will yield tangible results quickly.

Plan Elements

A city center development plan should contain three elements: a policy and objectives statement, an urban design framework, and a physical development plan. The successful revitalization in Lakeland, Florida, resulted from the planning process outlined in this chapter.

Policy and Objectives Statement

A clear statement of policies and objectives is the foundation for the city center development plan. The statement should express the basic goals for the city center in their simplest form without necessarily detailing how those goals are to be achieved or addressing the inherent tradeoffs necessary to obtain them.

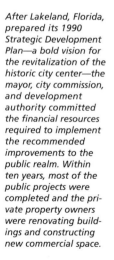

After Lakeland, Florida, prepared its 1990 Strategic Development Plan—a bold vision for the revitalization of the historic city center—the mayor, city commission, and development authority committed the financial resources required to implement the recommended improvements to the public realm. Within ten years, most of the public projects were completed and the private property owners were renovating buildings and constructing new commercial space.

158

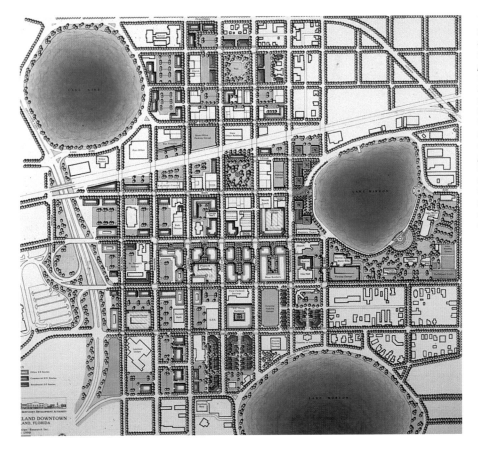

The development plan for the Lakeland city center identified all of the buildings worthy of preservation and renovation, and proposed new infill development for sites being used for surface parking. When the public realm improvement program commenced, private property owners began to renovate their buildings. Construction of two new parking decks made land available for new office and retail development.

Urban Design Framework

The urban design framework highlights the public sector elements that will establish the city center's physical organizing structure and outlines a plan of action for clarifying and strengthening these elements. The central area's street pattern, vehicular circulation, parking, transit system, network of pedestrian connections, streetscape, and open spaces all are addressed in this framework. These elements, which define the city center's public environment and image, are the same elements to which private development and investment will be attracted and around which that development will be organized. This development will help create the momentum necessary to sustain commitment and investment over the longer term.

Physical Development Plan

The city center physical development plan identifies opportunities and suggests desirable design solutions by showing how new development should relate to the urban design framework and existing development. The physical plan identifies city center subdistricts, and each subdistrict's landmarks, attractions, and key development sites. It also describes the preferred qualities for new development in terms of uses, building heights, overall massing, primary orientation, setbacks and build-to lines, pedestrian linkages, parking, and service access. By communicating the vision and physical development potential in the city center, a good plan becomes an effective basis for development negotiation and site plan review.

The Florida Department of Transportation constructed a roadway on the edge of Lake Mirror in Lakeland, cutting off valuable park land from the water. The 1990 development plan recommended removing the two-lane roadway and restoring the original pedestrian promenade conceived and constructed in the 1920s. Now, people once again enjoy the public promenade on the lake.

Plan Implementation Tools

Two categories of tools can be employed to implement a development plan: regulations and incentives, and design review.

Regulations and Incentives

Regulations governing development in the city center and incentives to promote private investment, which begin as proposals by the city's planning department or economic development department, become enforceable when they are adopted by city elected officials. Regulations can be applied through zoning codes, special district development ordinances, creation of planned unit development districts, and site plan review. Incentive zoning can be used to encourage developers to provide amenities in the center city.

Traditional Zoning Approaches. As long as it permits a mix of city center land uses, traditional as-of-right, or lot-by-lot, zoning can help advance many urban design objectives by controlling building heights, bulk and density, setback or build-to lines, and the location and treatment of parking, loading and service areas, landscaping, screening, and signage.

Nevertheless, as-of-right zoning tends to treat the entire city center district—or all

Master Plan Update
Downtown Lakeland
Lakeland, Florida

In 2002, Lakeland prepared an updated development plan to guide public and private investment over the next decade. One of the most important projects involves closing a second section of the state highway and extending the pedestrian promenade around the northern side of Lake Mirror. A two-story restaurant pavilion is proposed for the site overlooking the new extended lakefront park and promenade.

parcels of land in the same use class—uniformly. It fails to adequately recognize the differences in opportunities and constraints presented by individual parcels, or the different urban design objectives that may apply to particular subdistricts or development frontages, such as the pedestrian/retail spine. As a result, as-of-right zoning usually must be supplemented with special district ordinances, development codes, and design guidelines.

In addition, administration by the city of as-of-right zoning does not address effectively the need to coordinate the details of site-specific planning and design on adjacent parcels to maximize visual continuity

and functional integration. This kind of site coordination can best be provided through review of site or development plans based on adequate regulatory authority.

Special Districts. A special district ordinance or development code can be applied to an entire central area or to one or more of its subdistricts through overlay districts. Such an ordinance or code would require that a detailed physical plan be developed for the area so that it will attract or support specific initiatives intended to strengthen desirable physical characteristics and promote a set of more locally defined goals. The implementing ordinance also would

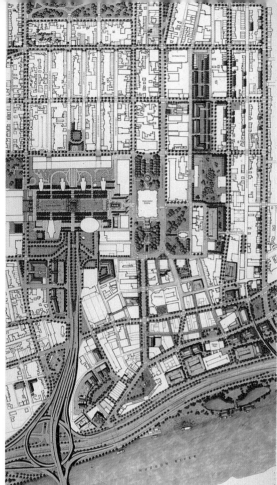

The development plan for the city center of Albany, New York, recommended rebuilding the public realm on State Street to enhance the pedestrian and vehicular approach to the state Capitol. State Street is the city's central spine, linking Capitol Hill to the Hudson River. Widened walkways and streetscape improvements will allow the restaurants to create outdoor cafés along this important civic street.

spell out in some detail the plan's urban design objectives and amenity requirements, as well as provide a review mechanism to ensure that new development is consistent with the area's special characteristics. By describing how development on individual lots should fit together to create a coordinated whole, the special district designation can help a central area overcome many of the shortcomings of traditional lot-by-lot, as-of-right zoning.

Planned Unit Development Districts.
Many cities have been able to achieve creative land use planning by creating planned unit development districts. Within these districts, which are planned as a whole, developers are permitted to transfer density between lots, subject to the district's overall plan, and to take advantage of greater flexibility in the overall site design. In return, the municipality gains more detailed review authority over the development plan and its design features.

Site Plan Review.
The review of site plans by the city staff and planning commission can be made mandatory before construction will be allowed for work planned anywhere in the community or in the central area, or applied only in special instances—for example, when increases in height or density are requested over what is permitted by the existing zoning. In any case, standards and criteria for approval of site plans must be carefully documented in advance and must be applied consistently and objectively.

Incentive Zoning.
Incentive zoning allows developers to earn bonuses of increased building height or development density in

162

return for the provision of desirable amenities. Incentive zoning is predicated on the assumption that the underlying zoning allows less development density than the market demands. Used wisely, incentive zoning provides a mechanism for promoting private sector cooperation in creating desirable public amenities and improvements such as plazas and parks. However, density bonus programs must be managed to ensure that their cumulative impact does not result in redundant amenities that do not benefit the public—e.g., a proliferation of plaza spaces that are not effectively used—or density increases that overwhelm infrastructure capacity.

Design Review

The design review process, which is usually advisory rather than mandatory, can address a range of issues, including the location and massing of buildings, their external impacts on surrounding areas, and their aesthetic character. Except where design review aims to preserve the architectural character of a historic area or other special district, it usually focuses primarily on functional issues, such as how the project fits with adjacent streets, walkways, open spaces, and buildings, rather than on detailed architectural design.

Like many zoning regulations, the design review can examine land uses; ground-

level programming; building orientation; setbacks and build-to lines; building height, bulk, and density; the provision of public amenities; signs; and the location and treatment of parking. Still important, but of secondary significance in most city center design review processes, are aesthetic and architectural concerns addressing building materials, colors and textures, facade proportions and details, the roof or cornice line, and architectural styles.

Design review, based on zoning regulations and illustrative guidelines adopted by the planning commission and city council, may become part of the developmental approval process administered by city staff—e.g., site plan review—or, it may be administered by an independent review board that advises the commission and council.

Because design guidelines are usually not mandatory, specific state enabling legislation may be required in some cases to allow a municipality to impose architectural design standards in areas outside designated historic districts.

Pearl Street, which has been the retail spine of Albany for many years, has been facing competition from new retail centers in the Albany region that offer customers a high-quality shopping environment. The only way merchants can compete with these new centers is to rebuild the Pearl Street public realm, renovate facades and storefronts, and finance new retail businesses that want to be in this revitalized shopping district.

163

More than any other city, more than any other region, the nation's capital should represent the finest in a living environment which America can plan and build.

—*John F. Kennedy*

Plan Implementation

The regeneration and development projects illustrated on the following pages were envisioned and designed based on the principles and guidelines set forth in the preceding chapters. Each of the 17 projects evolved from a comprehensive urban design plan and implementation strategy formulated by public and private sector leaders in the cities in which they are located.

Twelve of the selected projects are in large cities and five are in communities with a population of 75,000 to 150,000. Projects in Portland, Oregon, and Karlsruhe, Germany, were selected because these cities have designed and implemented public realm projects that have set a high standard for development in their central areas. The public realm improvements in the other cities were conceived by the author in collaboration with the clients and an interdisciplinary team of professionals.

The large cities are Baltimore, Maryland; Belfast, Northern Ireland; Chicago, Illinois; Cincinnati, Ohio; Karlsruhe, Germany; Liverpool, England; Manchester, England; Portland, Oregon; Washington, D.C.; and Wilmington, Delaware. The smaller cities are Cedar Rapids, Iowa; Kenosha, Wisconsin; Lakeland, Florida; Sarasota, Florida; and Savannah, Georgia.

Pennsylvania Avenue, Washington, D.C.

Baltimore, Maryland

INNER HARBOR DEVELOPMENT

Baltimore's Inner Harbor constitutes one of the most dramatic examples of successful city center regeneration. The development plan for the Inner Harbor recommended creating a waterfront promenade and a series of parks to encourage people to visit and enjoy recreation near the water. Development of the promenade and the green space demonstrated that a high-quality urban environment would attract people and stimulate private investment in offices, specialty retail, restaurants, hotels, and residential development.

A major pedestrian plaza with a water feature was developed on the northwest corner of the Inner Harbor to provide an appealing environmental connection between the waterfront and the office and commercial area north of Pratt Street. Wide, at-grade pedestrian crossings were created to encourage people to walk to the waterfront amenities and attractions.

Development of the waterfront public realm also set the tone for private investment in the residential neighborhoods west and south of the Inner Harbor. Revitalization of the historic residential areas has created life and vitality in the Inner Harbor and the heart of the city.

This page: Aerial view of pedestrian plaza and walkways that connect to the central core; entry plaza to the Inner Harbor; harbor promenade and retail pavilions; retail development in the power plant; south shore skating rink.

Facing Page: Illustrative drawing portraying the vision for the Inner Harbor; view of Inner Harbor marinas and skyline; waterfront open space after and before development.

Implementation: 1975 to 1995.

Baltimore, Maryland

OTTERBEIN NEIGHBORHOOD REGENERATION

The successful development of city center housing in Baltimore began with the revitalization of the Otterbein neighborhood west of the Inner Harbor and just south of the main office core. About 40 percent of this historic area had been cleared for a proposed high-density residential development project.

A revised urban design plan prepared by Charles Center Inner Harbor Management illustrated the potential of renovating 105 dwelling units and constructing an additional 50 units of attached housing. Exterior restoration guidelines were developed to assist the new homeowners in the architectural design of their facades; guidelines also were established for the infill development. Within two years, all of the existing structures were renovated, and the infill dwellings were completed within five years.

The city of Baltimore rebuilt the public infrastructure and created a series of small urban parks in the heart of each block. Brick walkways and historic lighting were introduced throughout the neighborhood. The city investment of about $3 million in public improvements generated more than $30 million in private investment.

This page: The project after and before infill development; completed townhouse project; sketch of the proposed townhouses; renovated facades and the front entry landscape.

Facing page: Aerial view of the neighborhood; renovated housing and the mature streetscape; sketch of streetscape improvements; vacant housing before redevelopment.

Implementation: 1978 to 1983.

Baltimore, Maryland

BOULEVARD DEVELOPMENT

The master plan for the city center of Baltimore recommended the construction of two major highways to provide access to the eastern and western sectors of the central area. A six-lane elevated roadway planned for the east side would have bisected a historic district. On the west side, a below-grade roadway was recommended to encircle the historic commercial district and provide direct access to Interstate 95 south of the central area.

Property owners and local preservationists challenged planners to evaluate roadway alternatives that would stimulate economic regeneration in the two historic districts. Maryland's preservation officer supported design studies illustrating the benefits of constructing boulevards that would respect historic properties and be sensitive to property owners in the existing neighborhood and commercial district.

Construction of the east side boulevard enhanced the value of properties in the Little Italy historic district and created a number of prime infill sites for private investment. Once the boulevard was completed, the city and state highway officials decided to build a second boulevard to serve as a gateway to the central area and the west side neighborhoods. This tree-lined roadway has stimulated investment in new housing and the regeneration of existing west side neighborhoods.

This page: South entrance to the city after and before redevelopment; pedestrian walkway and green parkway; east side boulevard in Little Italy after and before redevelopment.

Facing page: Sketch of the proposed boulevard; west side roadway and linear green space; roadway site before construction; boulevard-related residential development.

Implementation: 1977 to 1985.

Belfast, Northern Ireland

DONEGALL SQUARE ENHANCEMENT

The City Centre of Belfast reflects a classical form of development, with all roads leading to the City Hall. This magnificent building is surrounded by Donegall Square, the largest open space in the city center, which is enclosed by many impressive historic buildings that add to the importance of this public space.

Public realm improvements were designed to restore dignity to Donegall Square, with new ceremonial gates and a granite-paved courtyard providing an attractive forecourt for the City Hall. The granite walks and a granite curb, which replaced asphalt-paved walkways, serve as the border for rectangular grass panels that flank the entrance court and provide a relaxed setting for pedestrian activity.

This public realm enhancement project helped transform this historic open space into an important gathering place for the people of Belfast. In the blocks surrounding Donegall Square, retail activity also has prospered as a result of the improvements to this central space.

This page: Sketch of proposed improvements; public open space before improvement; people enjoying renovated green space; walkway paving and park furniture after and before improvements.

Facing page: Aerial view of the City Centre; sketch of proposed streetscape improvements; entry gate to City Hall; the street before improvements.

Implementation: 1990 to 1993.

Chicago, Illinois

ILLINOIS CENTER DEVELOPMENT

The 83-acre (34-hectare) Illinois Center air rights development, defined by Michigan Avenue, the Chicago River, Lake Michigan, and Grant Park, is one of the largest mixed-use projects in the United States. The pedestrian areas, plazas, and glass-enclosed public spaces were designed to preserve vistas to the river, the lakefront, and the park.

The primary pedestrian entrance to the development is from a plaza on Michigan Avenue, the major north-south image street of Chicago. One of the challenges faced by the design team involved creating a series of climate-controlled public spaces linked to a below-grade pedestrian walk system. The Hyatt Regency Hotel provided the opportunity to construct a large glass atrium with access to the lower-level walkways, creating an indoor activity area that, combined with other glass-enclosed spaces, has made the waterfront site enjoyable during the winter and on windy days.

The development site has accommodated more than 8 million square feet (743,000 square meters) of office and retail space, three hotels with 3,400 rooms, and 3,300 residential dwellings. Chicago receives about $80 million in tax revenues from the development in Illinois Center.

This page: Aerial view of Hyatt Regency Hotel complex; entrance courtyard to hotel; glass-enclosed dining and entertainment courtyards.

Facing page: Aerial view of lakefront marina, Grant Park, and Illinois Center; the entrance plaza off Michigan Avenue; outdoor café at Hyatt Regency Hotel; view of Illinois Center from Grant Park.

Implementation:
1971 to 1988.

175

Cincinnati, Ohio

CITY CENTER REGENERATION

The city of Cincinnati, in partnership with the private sector, has designed and developed several impressive public spaces in the heart of the city. One of the most successful urban plazas in the United States is Fountain Square, a central gathering place that is the focus of public activity and that has been the stimulus for private investment in the multiblock business district. The private sector has also planned and developed significant open-space amenities to enhance the public realm.

To stimulate residential development, Cincinnati redesigned Piatt Park, one of the city's oldest parks, as a catalyst for new housing. Changes to the two-block-long linear open space were planned in collaboration with private developers who were interested in investing in the historic Garfield Place neighborhood. A tree-lined park promenade was created to encourage pedestrian activity and to provide a positive environment for the new multistory residential development.

This page: Walkways and pedestrian amenities in the city center; Fountain Square Plaza; Procter and Gamble park and gardens; statue of President James A. Garfield in Piatt Park.

Facing page: Aerial view of the city center; Piatt Park promenade after and before improvements; new multistory residential development fronting the park; streetscape along new residential development.

Implementation: 1975 to 1985.

Karlsruhe, Germany

CITY CENTER REGENERATION

Karlsruhe, Germany, is one of the most beautiful cities in Europe. The public realm in the city center has been designed to encourage people to walk or bicycle to the central core from residential neighborhoods throughout the city, and the primary streets that serve adjacent communities have dedicated lanes for bicycles and light-rail transit, thus reducing dependence on the private automobile.

Most of the roadways and bicycle corridors follow historic rights-of-way that were conceived and developed in the 1700s. Thirty-two main avenues were built over the next 200 years, each radiating from the Palace Tower in the center of the city. The Palace Gardens, five minutes from the retail district by foot, offers a place for residents and visitors to relax, and a number of walks and bikeways radiate from the Palace Gardens to the Hardtwald Forest preserve.

The avenues, boulevards, and parks within the heart of the city provide a unifying environmental structure for the community and the region. The quality of life has been enhanced by the vision and commitment of the community leaders who designed and built this city's world-class public realm.

This page: Passive recreation space around the palace; formal park space that connects to the retail district; palace restaurant and café; horticultural gardens.

Facing page: Pedestrian walkway in the cultural area; light-rail transit line in the heart of the retail district; outdoor café in the central park; bicycle and pedestrian path that connects to the city center.

Implementation: 1975 to 1990.

Liverpool, England

CITY CENTER REGENERATION

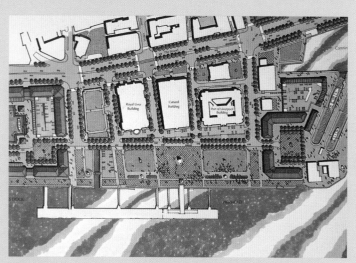

The historic center of Liverpool had many valuable assets upon which to base the creation of a world-class tourist destination. The English Tourist Board, in collaboration with the Liverpool City Council and the Merseyside Development Corporation, prepared a comprehensive development plan that focused on improving the public realm throughout the city center.

Within five years, two major pedestrian corridors were redesigned and reconstructed to improve visibility and vehicular access. Streets and pedestrian walkways connecting to the retail center were enhanced to encourage greater use of the dedicated public space in the city center.

The most dramatic change in the public environment occurred with the redesign and reconstruction of the historic Pierhead public space, reclaimed as a pedestrian area by eliminating parking lots and a bus terminal. A new granite-paved plaza and riverfront promenade were created for outdoor events including musical performances, festivals, and ceremonies. The improvements to the public realm stimulated private investment throughout the city center.

This page: Pedestrian plaza; plaza statue; Church Street retail corridor; two important public spaces in the city center.

Facing page: Sketch of the proposed park improvements for the Pierhead; the completed park; urban design plan for riverfront area; parking area before development.

Implementation: 1988 to 1992.

Manchester, England

BRIDGEWATER CANAL REGENERATION

The Bridgewater Canal District was the birthplace of the Industrial Revolution and the location of the United Kingdom's first urban heritage park. In an effort to promote and develop tourism in a 1,000-acre (405-hectare) area that includes the canal district, the English Tourist Board established a plan to renovate the historic canals and the river. This plan emerged as a key regeneration strategy because of its potential to provide a significant open-space amenity and sites for major development.

Initial emphasis was placed on enhancing the pedestrian environment with new opportunities for public access to and enjoyment of the existing waterways. Following implementation of public realm improvements, the private sector responded by providing a lively mix of pubs, restaurants, offices, residences, and leisure facilities.

A public/private development corporation was established to manage the design and construction in the project area. A £54 million (US$90 million) public commitment in infrastructure and development has generated more than £430 million (US$715 million) in private investment over a ten-year period.

This page: Perspective sketch of proposed improvements; canal area before improvements; renovated residential buildings; canal edge enhancements; a restaurant developed under the arches of the railroad viaduct.

Facing page: Aerial view of the city center; perspective sketch of canal district improvements: canal after and before redevelopment.

Implementation: 1988 to 1995.

Portland, Oregon

CITY CENTER REGENERATION

In the late 1960s, Portland was threatened by several devastating trends: deteriorating air quality, loss of housing, destruction of historic buildings and landmarks, and dwindling retail activity. Portland's leaders organized an effort to prepare a plan for regeneration of the city center by creating a dynamic urban core.

Initial planning and implementation focused on improving the public realm. A major highway along the river was removed to create a riverfront park, and in the center of the retail district, a number of buildings were removed to construct Pioneer Courthouse Square, a meeting place for local people and the site of many festivals and celebrations.

The pedestrian environment on the most important retail streets was enhanced to complement the improvements being made along the bus and light-rail transit corridors. The quality of the public realm improvements, combined with the introduction of public art, stimulated the private sector to invest in housing on the riverfront, a specialty retail center, hotels, and related commercial development throughout the central area.

In the past five years, more than 300,000 square feet (28,000 square meters) of new retail space has been added, providing a strong mix of national, local, and independent retailers. Development of about 5,000 housing units during the same period has created demand for three new parks in the central area. The success of the Portland program evolved from the city's vision and commitment to develop a high-quality, people-friendly city center.

This page: Pedestrian promenade and retail/residential housing; riverfront park development; Pioneer Courthouse Square public space; light-rail transit street; Ira Keller Fountain.

Facing page: Dedicated bus transitway; streetscape and furniture; retail stores and pedestrian amenities; boulevard landscape.

Implementation: 1975 to 1995.

Washington, D.C.

PENNSYLVANIA AVENUE REGENERATION

The urban design plan and guidelines for Washington's Pennsylvania Avenue recommended rebuilding the public realm between the U.S. Capitol and the U.S. Treasury Building. Congressional approvals made the design plan the guiding document for all redevelopment along this highly visible and symbolic street. An important aspect of the plan was creation of a comfortable pedestrian environment and an impressive setting for ceremonies and parades.

A major design proposal involved rerouting Pennsylvania Avenue between 12th and 14th streets in order to establish two public spaces intended to serve as a visual and functional terminus to the avenue. Those spaces, Pershing Park and Freedom Plaza, created a sense of place and stimulated investment in hotels, theaters, retail space, offices, and restaurants. Major private investment also occurred following creation of a public plaza between Seventh and Ninth streets, known today as the Navy Memorial Plaza.

The $149 million appropriated for Pennsylvania Avenue public improvements and development has generated more than $1.5 billion in private investment.

This page: Streetscape improvements; aerial view of eastern sector of Pennsylvania Avenue before redevelopment; Navy Memorial Plaza development; plaza fountain and amenities; outdoor cafés.

Facing page: Perspective sketch of proposed public realm improvements; streetscape enhancement and amenities; office building after and before restoration and development.

Implementation: 1975 to 1990.

Wilmington, Delaware

CHRISTINA RIVERFRONT DEVELOPMENT

Tubman Garrett Park, a formal public open space adjacent to the Wilmington train station, is one of the community focal points along the revitalized Christina Riverfront in Wilmington. The park provides a pedestrian link between the waterfront and the city center, and offers a setting for reflection, passive and active recreation, and historic interpretation.

The riverfront park, designed as a center of activity for festivals and events and as a year-round venue for public recreation, has as its focus a tree-lined crescent that provides clear views to the river. The materials selected for the park reflect many of the building materials used in turn-of-the-century Wilmington.

Tubman Garrett Park is located at a central point along the 1.5-mile (2.4-kilometer) riverwalk that links businesses, the new Riverfront Arts Center, the Shipyard Shops retail center, and a wildlife refuge. The resulting redevelopment of the riverfront has enlarged the tax base, added 800 jobs, and increased the number of resident and tourist visits. The public investment on the riverfront has stimulated private investment along the historic commercial corridors that link the heart of the city to the river.

This page: Riverfront promenade and landscape; riverfront open space; two views of riverfront before development; tree-lined crescent walkway.

Facing page: Perspective sketch of proposed riverfront improvements; riverfront after enhancement; entrance gateway; riverfront park site before improvements.

Implementation: 1996 to 2000.

Cedar Rapids, Iowa

CITY CENTER REGENERATION

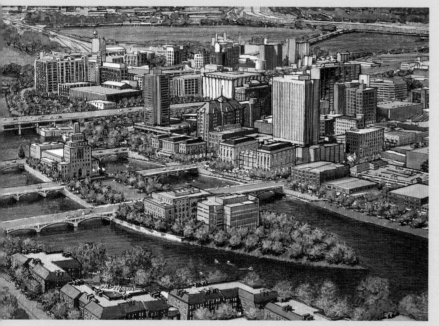

The revitalization strategy for the central area of Cedar Rapids focused on the enhancement of the public realm in a 48-block municipal improvement district. Implementation of this comprehensive streetscape improvement program has stimulated major private investment throughout the center of the city.

The urban design plans for the central area evolved from a series of meetings and work sessions with community leaders and property owners who were committed to development of a people-friendly environment. Walkways were widened along the Second Street corridor to provide adequate space for streetscape amenities and to improve pedestrian circulation at major intersections.

Property owners were assessed for special paving, street furniture, and landscape amenities; the public sector funded the cost of the concrete walks, curbs, lighting, and utilities. An investment of $16 million in public realm improvements has stimulated more than $54 million in private development.

This page: Perspective sketch of the planned retail store renovation; stores before improvements; completed store renovation; two views of Second Street corridor after improvements; Second Street before improvements.

Facing page: Aerial view of the riverfront and city center; perspective sketch of the area; pedestrian realm along Second Street retail corridor after enhancement; Second Street before improvement.

Implementation: 1988 to 1993.

Kenosha, Wisconsin

HARBORPARK DEVELOPMENT

In 1989, Kenosha began a ten-year planning process to redevelop 69 acres (28 hectares) of industrial land fronting Lake Michigan. To establish a definitive program for the site, the city engaged the Urban Land Institute (ULI) to evaluate the market potential of and to formulate a development strategy for the city's valuable lakefront property. The ULI Advisory Services report provided a concept upon which the city could base detailed plans for a new urban neighborhood.

The design plan for the site proposed extending the existing street grid eastward from the central business district. It also called for a system of parks and boulevards to provide access and view corridors to the water and to the heart of the city.

The open-space system provided the amenity that led to development of a high-quality residential area and the construction of the new Kenosha Public Museum on the central commons. Additional public buildings and a neighborhood retail center are planned for key locations along the parks and boulevards that have been developed by the city.

This page: Perspective sketch of waterfront promenade and park; waterfront before improvements; pedestrian promenade; perspective sketch of central commons and Kenosha Public Museum; commons after development.

Facing page: Aerial view of lakefront development area; waterfront development; three-story residential condominiums; light-rail transit corridor.

Implementation: 1997 to 2001.

Lakeland, Florida

HISTORIC DISTRICT REGENERATION

Lakeland formulated a vision for its future to encourage high-quality development while preserving and enhancing the city center's historic setting and natural environment. Evidence of this success can be seen in the city center public realm improvements, the Lake Mirror Park enhancement, and restoration of many historic landmarks.

The streetscape enhancement program has established a positive image for city center activity. Pedestrians enjoy the tree-shaded walks, colorful seasonal plantings, distinctive lights, and benches that line Lakeland's major streets.

Munn Park has become the central amenity space in the heart of the commercial district. Reconstruction and enhancement of this historic square has energized the area as a popular place to eat lunch or attend a festival or special event.

More than $80 million in private funds has been invested in the 35-block central area, and a total of $12 million in public funds has been committed to park and streetscape improvements.

This page: Kentucky Avenue after and before improvements; Munn Park after enhancement; Lake Mirror Park and promenade before and after improvements.

Facing page: Aerial view of the city center; perspective sketch of proposed development; Lemon Street before improvements; sketch of Lemon Street promenade improvements; enhanced streetscape.

***Implementation:** 1989 to 2002.*

Sarasota, Florida

CITY CENTER REGENERATION

In Sarasota, public forums held as part of a comprehensive planning process identified the need for a new central area public space. A triangular parcel of land was acquired by the city for the development of an activity plaza and green space, and the new Five Points Park was constructed within three years of completion of the plan. Removal of existing commercial buildings and development of the park stimulated new investment in the underused land to the north. This important open space provided the stimulus for the city and county to collaborate on the design and construction of a new central library.

The comprehensive plan for the Sarasota city center, which identified the need to create two new pedestrian walkways to connect the bayfront to the heart of the city, was used to convince the state highway department to install traffic signals on Bayfront Drive to permit pedestrians to cross the parkway at grade. On the bayfront, the parks were redesigned, as was the parking, to encourage greater use of this natural amenity and to provide an attractive gateway to the city center. The investment of public funds on the bayfront and in the heart of the city center has generated more than $750 million in private investment.

This page: Bayfront Drive after and before improvements; bayfront park enhancement; urban design plan for the bayfront and city center; pedestrian link to the bayfront.

Facing page: Perspective sketch of proposed improvements to Five Points Park; the park after enhancement; park site and public plaza after and before improvements.

Implementation: 1985 to 1992.

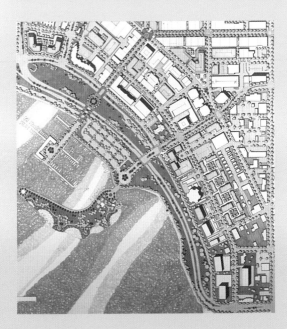

Savannah, Georgia

CITY CENTER REGENERATION

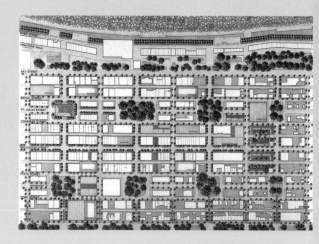

The proposed development plan for the central area of Savannah focused on enhancement of the public realm to stimulate private investment in the historic buildings in the commercial and residential heart of the city. Development of a high-quality streetscape on Broughton Street, Savannah's historic main street, provided an incentive for reinvestment in the commercial properties along this retail corridor and in the blocks to the north and south. Most of the historic landmarks in this district have been renovated and recycled for office, hotel, educational, or institutional use.

Revitalization of the older residential neighborhoods located south of the commercial district has benefited from the environmental enhancement of the historic park squares. Six of the squares were redesigned and rebuilt to generate private investment in the hundreds of residential properties that define the squares, tree-lined streets, and boulevards.

The value of commercial real estate in the city center has grown by $80 million over the past 15 years, and more than $1 billion of income is generated annually from tourists visiting the Savannah area.

This page: Forsyth Park promenade; Whitefield Square before improvements; Whitefield Square after enhancement; activities in two restored park squares.

Facing page: Urban design plan for the city center; Orleans Square; Broughton Street storefronts today; Broughton Street before and after revitalization.

Implementation: 1975 to 1995.

A city should be a place with such beauty and order that it is inspirational ... the greatest cities are those with the most beautiful places.

—Joseph Riley

Conclusion

Successful city centers do not just happen. Nor are they necessarily the result of fortuitous history, geography, or economics. They come about because individuals and agencies within the public and private sectors make decisions and take a series of actions.

Many cities have effected substantial change through concerted public and private efforts, but no easy formula or surefire method exists that guarantees development of a successful city center. Each city is different, each has its own assets, liabilities, personality, and opportunities, and each will have its own path to and definition of success.

Still, a study of city center success stories reveals some shared general precepts and key elements. The most important lesson provided by a review of successful city centers is that substantial change can be brought about through the concerted actions of government agencies and private citizens.

City centers that two decades ago seemed stagnant are now lively, busy hearts of their cities, with new investment, jobs, businesses, residents, and a sense of pride among those who live and work there.

Centennial Square, West Palm Beach, Florida.

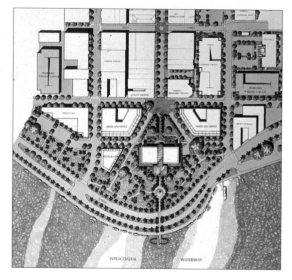

The preliminary design plans for the retail and waterfront area in West Palm Beach motivated community leaders to work together to establish a clearly defined vision for the heart of the city. The private investment that has been generated from this vision is a testament to the value of the visioning process.

But for every glittering success, there is an example of a failed effort—of the continuing exodus of retail and other businesses from the center city, and of a failed project that was intended to be the beginning of the central area renaissance.

How do cities and towns begin the process of developing a successful city center? Though examples can be cited where central area revitalization began with a private sector or business community initiative, it is critical that the public sector—city government—play a key role throughout the entire regeneration process.

The starting point is the creation and articulation of a vision for the city center. The vision must be broad and ambitious to inspire and energize the community. It must be comprehensive enough to ensure the success of the city center. And, at the same time, it must recognize limits and focus on those aspects of the city center that can be managed.

Though the need for a comprehensive vision seems self-evident, lack of such a vision of the new city center is often the principal stumbling block in the process. It is of paramount importance that cities seeking to protect or revive their centers look far into the future to envision the greatest potential that can be achieved. Too often, opportunities are compromised or overlooked at the outset by negative thinking or the inability to let go of the status quo. This is not the stage at which to be impeded by trivial issues or negative thinking.

Realization of the vision will require the enthusiastic support and participation of many forces throughout the city and surrounding area. When city government takes the lead in creating a vision of the successful city center, the eventual widespread and constructive involvement of other sectors of the community is essential.

Because most city government agencies are overwhelmed by current operations

202

and assignments, the city government puts the city center vision at risk if it assigns the task of regeneration to an existing government agency or agencies without providing the organization, staff, funding, and authority necessary to perform the job. Many successful urban regeneration projects have been led by separate, quasi-private agencies created specifically to carry out the city center vision. Such agencies often are empowered with broad entrepreneurial capabilities that permit them to engage in negotiations and deal making with private sector entities. When dealing with the complex issues of larger city centers, creation of such special agencies may be especially important. All such agencies should have clear lines of authority and should be supported financially by the city government.

Many of the guidelines and criteria contained in this volume apply to the creation of the vision for the city center and

its implementation. These tasks must involve city planning departments and other agencies, along with outside planners, economic and market researchers, urban designers, architects, landscape architects, and other key professionals.

The future of the city center must be a concern of the entire community. Still, much of the essential drive and energy will come from the people who are willing to provide the leadership, ideas, ingenuity, and persistence to shape their community and its future.

The principal test of the successful city center is the extent to which it is used by

On Clematis Street in West Palm Beach, the city center's retail spine, building facades and storefronts were renovated, walkways were widened, and two-way traffic was restored. Within five years, all of the historic buildings were released to commercial tenants.

The main entrance to the city library was cluttered with newspaper vending machines and traffic signals. To stimulate investment in the adjacent blocks, the development authority constructed an interactive fountain at the visual terminus of Clematis Street.

its residents and visitors, the frequency with which they use it, and the degree of satisfaction they derive from it. Both residents and visitors are drawn to a city center that offers entertainment, variety, and the enjoyment of a busy, attractive, diverse, and comfortable place. The heart of the city can become the best advertisement for and an open door to new investment, new business, and new ideas.

A successful city center is not beyond the reach of any city, regardless of its size, location, or history. The road may be long and difficult and the obstacles may seem insurmountable. Short-term success may be limited by the many demands for innovation, creative financing, leadership, community participation, and faith in the future. But where even a small urban spark can be ignited, the process can begin.

The requirements and costs of energizing the central area to achieve its full potential must be measured against the benefits of added tax base, jobs, business activity, and other residual benefits to the community. The basic costs often seem staggering, but if they are spread over a reasonable period of time, if the economic benefits are understood, and if early successes

The land north of the city library was occupied by one-story commercial buildings and surface parking lots. Those structures were replaced by five-story residential buildings, developed privately in response to the city's investment in the public realm. The new housing, as well as adjacent restaurants and retail shops and a nearby restored theater, all contribute to the vitality of this special place.

Residents and visitors value and enjoy the life and vitality generated by a well-designed and well-maintained space in West Palm Beach in the same way that New Yorkers appreciate and enjoy Bryant Park. Every city, large or small, deserves to have one or more public spaces that enrich and enhance quality of life.

can be secured, community support for an action program will be forthcoming. This is especially true if it is clear that the alternative is likely to be continued disinvestment in the city center and the debilitating impact it will have on the community as a whole.

Today, unlike two decades ago, the promise of city center regeneration is more credible. Much is owed to urban visionaries such as Edmund Bacon, Jane Jacobs, Sen. Daniel Patrick Moynihan, James Rouse, and William H. Whyte who ignored the pessimism and spoke out for a new vision of how the city center can enrich our lives and our communities as a whole. Thanks to them, we can pursue our visions with greater confidence and determination.

Good practice in urban regeneration and innovation around the world demonstrate the importance of thinking, planning, and acting creatively in addressing urban issues.

—Charles Landry

Resources

For those wishing to pursue the subject of successful city center development in greater depth, additional assistance is available.

The Urban Land Institute, through its staff, publications, and meetings, makes available material and case studies on virtually every aspect of urban development and regeneration. Expertise on city center management, urban revitalization, and marketing is available from the International Downtown Association, an organization that serves business improvement districts, urban development agencies, and consultants in the United States and Canada, and abroad. The National Trust for Historic Preservation, through its Main Street Program, publications, and other activities, also offers a wealth of material, case histories, and expertise. Many cities and towns that have implemented successful city center regeneration programs are pleased to share their experiences with others. Organizations such as the American Institute of Architects, American Planning Association, American Society of Landscape Architects, and Association of Town Center Management in the United Kingdom have developed extensive resources on subjects pertinent to city center design and development.

Photo and Graphic Credits

With the exception of those identified below, all the photographs appearing in this book are from the author's private collection. Other photographs and graphics are used with the permission of the following people and organizations:

James Abbott—Bryant Park, New York City.

Fred Jarvis—the Champs-Elysées, Paris.

Patrick Mullaly—Lakeshore Drive, Chicago.

Jerry Johnson—aerial view of Illinois Center, Chicago.

Martin Luther King, Jr., Memorial Library—historic photographs of Washington, D.C.

National Capital Planning Commission—aerial view of the White House and Lafayette Park.

Eric Hyne, Encore Arts—perspective sketches of urban design projects.

Tishman Speyer Properties—Potsdamer Platz.